Feminism and Pornography

Feminism and
PORNOGRAPHY

Ronald J. BERGER,
Patricia SEARLES,
and Charles E. COTTLE

PRAEGER

New York
Westport, Connecticut
London

Copyright Acknowledgments

The author and publisher are grateful to the following for allowing the use of excerpts from:

Berger, Ronald J., Patricia Searles, and Charles E. Cottle. 1990. "A camp divided: Feminists on pornography." Pp. 67–102 in G. Miller and J. Holstein (eds.), *Perspectives on Social Problems*. Volume 2. Greenwich, CT: JAI Press, Inc.

Berger, Ronald J., Patricia Searles, and Charles E. Cottle. 1990. "Ideological contours of the contemporary pornography debate: Divisions and alliances." *Frontiers: A Journal of Women Studies* 11, no. 2: 30–38. Copyright © by Frontier Editorial Collective.

Cottle, Charles E., Patricia Searles, Ronald J. Berger, and Beth Ann Pierce. 1989. "Conflicting ideologies and the politics of pornography." *Gender and Society* 3, no. 3 (September): 303–33. Copyright © 1989 by Sociologists for Women in Society. Used by permission of Sage Publications, Inc.

Library of Congress Cataloging-in-Publication Data

Berger, Ronald J.
    Feminism and pornography / Ronald J. Berger, Patricia Searles, and
    Charles E. Cottle.
      p.   cm.
    Includes bibliographical references and index.
    ISBN 0-275-93819-0 (alk. paper)
      1. Pornography—Social aspects.   2. Feminism.   3. Obscenity (Law).
    I. Searles, Patricia.   II. Cottle, Charles E.   III. Title.
    HQ471.B47   1991
    363.4′ 7—dc20   90-24125

British Library Cataloguing in Publication Data is available.

Library of Congress Catalog Card Number: 90-24125
ISBN: 0-275-93819-0

First published in 1991

Praeger Publishers, One Madison Avenue, New York, NY 10010
An imprint of Greenwood Publishing Group, Inc.

Printed in the United States of America

The paper used in this book complies with the
Permanent Paper Standard issued by the National
Information Standards Organization (Z39.48-1984).

10 9 8 7 6 5 4 3 2 1

Contents

Preface

In the last two decades there has been a virtual explosion of literature on sexuality and sexual violence, much of which has been written from a feminist perspective. In the 1980s pornography emerged as a hotly debated issue among both feminists and nonfeminists. In this book, we synthesize the literature on pornography that has been written from a *feminist* perspective. The uniqueness of our approach lies in the framing of the topic in terms of the debate among feminists, while also reviewing much of the nonfeminist literature on pornography. Our goal has been to maintain a balanced approach to the feminist debate. We attempt to allow the many voices of feminism to speak for themselves, and rather than arguing for one point of view, to offer even-handed criticism of the limitations of the different feminist perspectives.

While the book will be of interest to graduate students and scholars in the field, it is written in a style designed to make the ideas accessible to upper-level undergraduate students as well. The book can be used as a "special topics" text in undergraduate and graduate courses in women's studies, gender studies, sexuality, social problems, deviance, criminology, and law.

We would like to thank Mary Glenn, our editor at Praeger Publishers, for her support of this project. We would also like to thank Alda Trabucchi, our project editor, and Bruce Cleary, our copy editor.

Feminism and Pornography

1

The Feminist Movement and the Contemporary Pornography Debate

In the 1980s pornography emerged as one of the most hotly contested social issues, and one that divided the feminist community. Both antipornography feminists and political conservatives decried the harm caused by pornography and proposed various, though differing, political and legal remedies. The U.S. Attorney General's Commission on Pornography (1986)—the Meese Commission—called for increased prosecutions under existing obscenity laws, as well as the passage of new laws against pornography. Liberals and civil libertarians within and outside the feminist community challenged this political agenda, charged the antipornography movement with advocating censorship, and warned of the negative consequences of increased governmental involvement in this issue.

Neither contemporary conservatives nor liberals or civil libertarians have advanced new ideas in the pornography debate. The former view pornography as a threat to the family and the moral fabric of society, while the latter are concerned that legal restrictions on pornography would infringe upon First Amendment rights to freedom of speech and expression. What is new in the debate are the opposing feminist analyses and politics regarding the problem of violence against women and regarding the nature of sexuality and its representation. While antipornography feminists, concerned about violence against women, have developed a theory and politics that focus on the harm caused by pornography, other feminists have emphasized the potentially beneficial effects of pornography as well as the dangers of censorship (Berger et al. 1990a).

The debate among feminists reached its most heated and polarized form when it centered around the antipornography civil rights ordinance first introduced by Andrea Dworkin and Catharine MacKinnon in Minneapolis in 1983. According to Dworkin and MacKinnon (1988), the ordinance was intended to empower women by giving them the option of civil suit against those whose involvement with pornography caused harm to women.[1] Feminists concerned about censorship responded by forming the Feminist Anti-Censorship Taskforce (FACT), an organization that helped develop a successful legal challenge to the constitutionality of a similar civil rights ordinance passed in Indianapolis in 1984 (see *American Booksellers Association, Inc. v. Hudnut* 1984; Baldwin 1986; Hunter & Law 1985). Although some feminists had reservations about both the FACT and Dworkin-MacKinnon positions, the Indianapolis case forced many to take sides, and the exchanges between them often took a particularly personal character that shattered some feminists' vision of sisterhood (see MacKinnon 1985; Rich 1985; Van Gelder 1986). While Lisa Duggan, Nan Hunter, and Carole Vance (1985) argued that the civil rights approach was "dangerous" in its attempt to "embody in law an analysis . . . of sexuality and sexual images . . . with which . . . all feminists do not agree" (p. 151), Dworkin asserted that women were "collaborating with male power" if they were not "working for [their] sisters" in favor of the ordinance and other antiviolence efforts (quoted in Bader 1987, p. 2; see Berger et al. 1990b).

GENDER AND PUBLIC OPINION
ON PORNOGRAPHY

Early in the debate, antipornography feminists envisioned a united feminist opposition to pornography (Russell 1980). They assumed that once feminists took a close look at pornography they would understand its pernicious nature, even if they differed on strategies and tactics. The current divisions among feminists have shattered any hoped-for solidarity. Indeed, antipornography feminists seriously underestimated the extent to which other women would be opposed to an antipornography political agenda.

The expectation of an antipornography consensus among feminists may have originated, in part, from the belief that the differential location of women and men in the social structure would inevitably lead them to hold different views about pornography. This expectation was supported by data from national surveys, such as the General Social Survey conducted by the National Opinion Research Center, which indicated that women were less likely than men to have seen an X-rated movie, and that they were more likely to agree that pornography has negative effects and to disagree that it has positive effects (Davis & Smith 1986; see *Time* 1986). Similarly, Pauline Bart, Linda Freeman, and Peter Kimball (1985) found that women evaluated the issue along different dimensions than men. For example, women's support for a pluralistic society tolerant of pornography was more contingent than men's on whether they believed pornography caused harm to women. Although some women and men agreed that "pornography has its place," Bart et al. argued that "variation among women is not mostly about whether they like pornography; they do not. They dislike it. But some feel ideologically called upon to tolerate what they can never like in order not to feel marked as an enemy of liberty, or perhaps to gain approval from men. On the other hand, men who say that porn has its place are more likely actually to approve [of] it" (p. 315).

Other survey research suggests, however, that Bart et al. may have overstated the case in asserting that "there are no 'community standards' [regarding pornography]—there are male standards and female standards" (p. 319). According to the General Social Survey, a majority of *both* men and women agreed that pornography has positive as well as negative effects (Davis & Smith 1986; see *Time* 1986). For instance, half or more of both genders agreed not only that pornography causes "a breakdown of morals" (55 percent of men and 67 percent of women) and leads "people to commit rape" (50 percent and 61 percent, respectively), but also that it provides "useful information about sex" (60 percent and 55 percent, respectively) as well as "an outlet for bottled-up impulses" (61 percent and 58 percent, respectively). In addition, while 64 percent of men opposed laws prohibiting the distribution of pornography to adults, so did 44 percent of women. Moreover, women accounted for about 40 percent of X-rated video rentals (Leo 1987), and nearly half the women responding to a *Redbook* magazine survey said they regularly watched pornographic films (Rubenstein & Tavris 1987).

The surveys suggest that although women are generally less favorable than men to pornography, there is no uniform "female" or "male" view.[2] Views on pornography are influenced by a number of factors in addition to gender—religious orientation, age, race, education, occupation, geographic region, and urban-rural location. For instance, in their analysis of General Social Survey data, Michael Wood and Michael Hughes (1984) found that female, older, and less educated respondents held more antipornography attitudes, as did those who lived in the South and rural areas, those who were Catholic or members of a conservative Protestant religious denomination, and those who were employed in manual or lower white-collar occupations. Similarly, in a survey conducted in the Atlanta metropolitan area, Margaret Herrman and Diane Bordner (1983) found that male, black, younger, more educated, less religious, and less morally rigid respondents had more tolerant and favorable personal attitudes toward pornography (see Burton 1989; Cottle et al. 1989)

THE WOMEN'S MOVEMENT AND THE
FEMINIST ANTIVIOLENCE CAMPAIGN

Since there are differences among women, and even feminists, on the pornography issue, it is helpful to situate these disagreements in the context of the women's movement more generally. The contemporary women's movement emerged from the general social discontent and protests of the 1960s to become a major political force in the United States, and it has "profoundly changed the agenda of American politics by raising a series of new issues" concerning economics, family relations, reproduction, and sexuality (Boneparth & Stoper 1988, p. 1). By the late 1970s the movement had been successful in converting many of these "issues into actual changes in public policies in the form of new laws, judicial decisions and executive implementation."

Today's movement differs from earlier women's movements in that it has developed a diverse membership, a decentralized organizational structure, and a wide range of objectives and strategies (Chafe 1977).[3] In Luther Gerlach and Virginia Hine's (1970) terms, the contemporary movement can be described as segmentary, polycephalous, and reticulate. In other words, it is composed of multiple groups of varying sizes and scope, competing leaders, and a loose network of intersecting or overlapping members and branches (see Tierney 1982). Margarita Papandreou (1988) describes the women's movement as "a loosely knit federation of women's organizations, working in resistance to humiliation, inequality, and injustice" (p. xii). The *feminist* branch of this movement "embodies the awareness of the special oppression and exploitation that all women face as a gender group . . . [and] the willingness to organize and fight against women's subjugation in society and for the elimination of *sex-based injustice*."

One major focus of the feminist branch has been the problem of violence against women. Several relatively autonomous yet overlapping issues have been involved, including rape, incest, battering, sexual harassment, and self-defense, as well as pornography (see Lederer 1980; MacKinnon 1979; Rose 1977;

Russell 1984; Searles & Berger 1987; Tierney 1982). By the
mid-1970s, as Laura Lederer observed (1980):

Feminists . . . began to realize that although we must deal directly
with acute . . . problems like rape and wife-beating, we must also
remove the images which promote a climate in which these crimes
are possible. We noted the inconsistency in allowing (and even en-
couraging) women and young girls to be set up as sexual objects
and willing victims in all forms of mass media, while at the same
time protesting the victimization of females in real life. We began to
make the connections between media violence to women and real-life
violence to them, to recognize the threat which pornography poses
to our lives and livelihood, and to speak out against it. (pp. 16–17)

Robin Morgan (1980) encapsulated this view in her now-famous
antipornography slogan: "Pornography is the theory, and rape the
practice" (p. 139).

The feminist branch of the women's movement, however,
has not been without internal dissension and conflict over priorities, strategies, and tactics (Ryan 1989), although these differences have often been set aside to form coalitions to support abortion rights, the Equal Rights Amendment (ERA), and
various antidiscrimination policies (Boneparth & Stoper 1988;
Mansbridge 1986; Staggenborg 1986, 1988). Indeed, some degree
of disunity was inevitable given the diversity and organizational
fragmentation of the movement. In the 1980s the question of
pornography emerged as an area where disagreement among
feminists became highly pronounced. As we indicated above, the
feminist critique of pornography and support for antipornography
civil rights laws created strident opposition from anticensorship
feminists.

The divisions over pornography occurred in the context of a
broader controversy regarding the nature of sexuality that had
been brewing between radical and libertarian feminists since the
mid-1970s (Cohen 1986; Ferguson 1984; Freedman & Thorne
1984; Russo 1987). Radical feminists emphasized sexuality as
a social arena of victimization and oppressive inequality for

women, while libertarian feminists emphasized sexuality as an arena of constructive struggles toward women's sexual liberation. Radical feminists viewed pornography (along with rape, incest, and battering) as a form of violence against women, and attempted to establish antipornography politics as a priority for the women's movement. Libertarian feminists, on the other hand, accused radical feminists of promoting a "politics of despair" and a negativistic emphasis on women's victimization. They saw antipornography efforts as an attempt to revitalize the feminist movement in the wake of both the ERA's defeat and the declining economic status of women. And they considered it a misdirected strategy designed to attract conservative women to the feminist cause (Burstyn 1985b; Snitow 1985). But whereas conservative women were sympathetic to feminist antiviolence and antipornography efforts, they supported a broader conservative social and political agenda that was antagonistic to other feminist goals. For example, they defended traditional gender roles and family arrangements and opposed legalized abortion and the ERA (see Chafetz & Dworkin 1987; Dworkin 1983; Klatch 1987; Marshall 1989). Libertarian feminists thus feared that antipornography politics would promote a climate of sexual repression that would stifle women's sexual liberation (see Berger et al. 1990a, 1990b).

Libertarian and other anticensorship feminists cautioned antipornography feminists to heed the lessons of history (Burstyn 1985b). They noted that earlier nineteenth- and twentieth-century feminists in the United States, Great Britain, and Canada had been co-opted by conservative (often male-dominated) "social purity" movements that had favored restrictions on female sexuality and rejected women's right to control their own bodies and "seek sexual satisfaction outside religiously sanctioned patriarchal marriage" (p. 12).

For instance, nineteenth-century feminist efforts to rescue girls and women from prostitution stemmed from objections to the "double standard" of sexual morality and involved attempts to repeal the Contagious Disease Acts that stigmatized and isolated prostitutes and made it more difficult for them to move out of prostitution.[4] Feminists also desired to improve the educational and employment opportunities of women so they would not be dependent upon marriage or forced into prostitution for survival (Jones 1980). And they supported greater control by women of their bodies and asserted women's right of "self-defence against venereal disease, . . . overbearing male sexual demands, and excessive pregnancies" (Weeks 1981, p. 163). But in their efforts to translate their broader goals into law, feminists found it necessary to align themselves with nonfeminist, religious-based moral reformers who did not favor the economic and social independence of women. These advocates of "social purity" were more interested in protecting female virtue, returning women to their traditional roles, and preserving the patriarchal family. Whereas feminists wished to protect the individual liberty of women and prevent their sexual exploitation, the purity crusaders condemned all prostitutes except the young, innocent victims who could be "saved" from immoral debauchery and returned to a "pure" life (Barry 1979). As the movement became dominated by these nonfeminist moral reformers, it increasingly focused "on the victim and the need to uplift her" rather than on organized prostitution and the third parties who profited from the exploitation of women (p. 30).

By the end of the nineteenth century, the coalition of feminist and "social purity" activists had succeeded in achieving the repeal of the Contagious Disease Acts, raising the legal age of consent from twelve to sixteen years, and passing anti-obscenity legislation that essentially drove the pornography market underground.[5] In 1904, twelve countries ratified the International Agreement for the Suppression of the White Slave Traffic, thereby agreeing to take action against the "procuring of women and girls for immoral purposes abroad" (Barry 1979, p. 33). In 1910, the United States passed the Mann Act, which forbade transporting a female across either state lines or international boundaries for prostitution or other "immoral purposes." But Kathleen Barry notes that "the ambiguous term 'immoral purposes' suggests the extent to which the purity movement had succeeded in becoming the lawful guardian of female virtue. The question of women's will [was] entirely excluded from consideration and therefore the issue of individual liberty, so central to [feminists], was entirely lost in the language of the act" (p. 33).

Varda Burstyn (1985b), representing the libertarian/anticensorship side of the contemporary pornography debate, believes that these and other early legislative reforms, won through collaboration and compromise with nonfeminist and antifeminist forces, entailed high costs for women. As she writes:

The majority of women continued to be excluded in meaningful terms from public life and the political process. . . . Surveillance and persecution of all those who lived outside the standards of heterosexual marriage . . . increased. . . . 'Female chastity'—no sex except under conditions of marriage and procreation . . . —became the standard by which all other sexual practices were judged. . . . [And] the idea that the state should intervene in sexual life became accepted and stamped with women's approval. (pp. 12–14)

Although radical and other antipornography feminists do not deny the co-optation of earlier feminist campaigns (see Barry 1979), they do not believe these lessons of history should lead feminists to minimize women's experience of victimization and leave them unprotected by law (Cole 1989; Dworkin & MacKinnon 1988). They argue that the civil rights approach they propose would not increase state control but would instead empower women by giving them the ability to initiate civil litigation. Antipornography feminists are also critical of the alliance that anticensorship feminists have formed with both liberals (including the publishers of *Playboy* and *Penthouse*) and libertarians. Donna Greschner (1985) asks, "What evidence do we have that undesirable results will not be produced by these allegiances?" (p. 66). Antipornography feminists answer that liberals place freedom of speech above the protection of women, and that libertarians oppose virtually all state intervention, including that which would improve women's status—for example, affirmative action (MacKinnon 1987; see McCormack 1985a).

OVERVIEW AND PERSPECTIVE OF THE BOOK

Our primary aim in this book is to examine the feminist debate and synthesize the literature on pornography that has been written from a feminist perspective. This perspective, as this chapter has made clear, does not consist of a uniform point of view. Moreover, the feminist debate has taken place alongside much nonfeminist scholarly and political activity. While we do not intend this book as a comprehensive guide to the nonfeminist literature, we will situate the feminist debate in this broader context (see Donnerstein et al. 1987; Hawkins & Zimring 1988; Osanka & Johann 1989).

In Chapter 2 we preface our analysis of feminism and pornography by discussing traditional views on pornography that are embodied in popular opinion and governmental commissions. In Chapter 3 we examine radical and libertarian feminist perspectives on pornography and sexuality, and in Chapter 4 we evaluate other feminist perspectives that have not yet been as central to the pornography debate: liberal, Marxist, socialist, and black feminism. In Chapter 5 we consider men's perspectives on pornography and men's responses to the feminist debate. In Chapter 6 we assess the feminist debate in terms of the empirical research on pornography. Finally, in Chapter 7 we examine feminist and nonfeminist legal strategies, and in Chapter 8 we consider nonlegal alternatives.

Before considering *our approach* to the pornography issue, we briefly review other sociological approaches to this topic. One predominant sociological explanation of the antipornography movement in the United States has been characterized as the *status discontent* or *symbolic politics* approach (McConahay 1988; Zurcher & Kirkpatrick 1976). According to this view, supporters of "moral reform" movements (for example, temperance, antipornography) are reacting to frustration over actual or perceived declining social status (Gusfield 1963). Their discontent is expressed as outrage toward external groups whose behaviors or lifestyles embody a perceived threat to the social order. Concerns about restricting "immoral" behaviors are thus merely substitutes or symbols that focus supporters' attention on a tangible problem and make it appear that they are doing something to preserve their desired way of life.

One problem with this explanation of moral reform movements, as Wood and Hughes (1984) have shown, is that it discounts the role of cognitive processes or moral beliefs that are independent of status discontent. In their analysis of General Social Survey data, Wood and Hughes found that indicators of status discontent or declining social status were not related to attitudes toward pornography, suggesting that views about pornography were not necessarily symbolic of "something else." Instead, Wood and Hughes found that indicators of socialization or cultural experiences (such as age, religion, education, and residential location) were related to pornography. They argued that views on pornography were therefore related to learned beliefs and particular cultural environments and that no special theory of status discontent or frustration was required to account for antipornography attitudes (see Page & Clelland 1978).

Wood and Hughes's emphasis on beliefs and cultural factors is also supported by those who stress the importance of studying the beliefs or *ideology* of social movements in their own right (Downey 1986; Tucker 1989). The concept of ideology has numerous interpretations (Hunt 1985; Sumner 1979; Thompson 1984). We define it as publicly standardized collective representations or shared symbolic systems used by individuals to make sense of their world and from which their social action is informed and directed. We do not define ideology as irrational belief or false consciousness, and while we may be critical of particular perspectives, we are not primarily concerned with establishing the truth or falsity of a given point of view. Of course, some ideologies dominate others through their institutionalization in ongoing social, political, and legal practices (Althusser 1971), and feminist ideologies generally operate at the margin of mainstream institutions, if at all.

Ideologies, whether dominant or marginal, enable individuals to combine elements of thought (for example, concepts, ideas, beliefs, theories of social structure and politics) into a coherent world-view or value-laden perspective that is linked to social action.[6] At the same time, ideologies are often taken for granted and constraining, both logically and psychologically (Converse 1964). As such, they may limit thinking, blind participants to alternative points of view, and result in communicative distortions. In the feminist pornography debate, individuals representing different ideological perspectives have at times seemed to harden their positions, caricature their opponents, and make essentialist arguments (that is, claims about pornography's "essential" nature) that rule out any middle ground (see Diamond & Quinby 1984; Ferguson 1984; Philipson 1984).

This polarization has been characteristic of the feminist movement as a whole (Ryan 1989). As is often the case with social movements, participants have difficulty overlooking relatively minor within-group differences. Instead of producing unity, common membership creates "intense in-group antagonism . . . [and] factionalism" that threatens the movement's success (pp. 239–40; see Gamson 1975). Georg Simmel, a classic theorist of group conflict, noted that "people who have many common features often do one another worse . . . than complete strangers do. . . . They do this because there is only little that is different between them: hence even the slightest antagonism has a relative significance. . . . The divergence over a very insignificant point makes itself felt in its sharp contrast as something utterly unbearable" (1971, p. 91).

Barbara Ryan (1989) argues that the process of polarization in the feminist movement became tied up with participants' self-identity or very "definition of themselves" (p. 243). Contemporary feminist activists moved "from introducing new ways of seeing to a narrowed view of feminist legitimacy" that established competing views of "correct thinking" and turned "disputes over theory . . . into disputes over who was the most . . . or . . . the right kind of feminist" (pp. 245, 252). Rather than producing "creative dialogue" or self-critical examination, feminist theory at times became an obstacle to the coalition-building necessary for political success (see Nicholson 1989).

While we do not claim to have discovered the "middle ground" that might unite feminists dealing with the pornography issue, we attempt to mediate the arguments in a reasonably balanced fashion. Although an *objectivist* approach to social problems would view them as "objective and identifiable societal conditions that have intrinsically harmful effects," a *social constructionist* approach would define them as the product of "activities of individuals or groups making assertions of grievances and claims with respect to some putative condition" (Hilgartner & Bosk 1988, p. 53; Spector & Kitsuse 1977, p. 75; Hazelrigg 1986). According to this latter view, "statements about social problems . . . select a specific interpretation of reality from a plurality of possibilities. Which 'reality' comes to dominate public discourse has profound implications for the future of the social problem, for the interest group involved, and for policy" (Hilgartner & Bosk 1988, p. 58). Social constructionist studies, for example, point out that it has only been in the last three decades that social practices such as child abuse, wife-battering, and sexual harassment have attracted public attention and acquired the status of "social problems" (see Benson & Thompson 1982; Pfohl 1977; Tierney 1982).

Without denying the reality of people's suffering (Eitzen 1984; Quinney 1989), we believe the issue of pornography cannot be understood by focusing simply on "objective" conditions. We recognize that "pornography" is an ambiguous term, that people refer to different imagery when they use the word. Indeed, both laypeople and academics often quibble over definitions— about what pornography *is* and what it *does* (that is, its effects). However, Michael Kimmel (1990) argues that the belief that we need a common "definition that will hold across all cases is one of the major barriers that prevents various groups from speaking with each other" (p. 306).

We are not going to offer an operational definition that some would inevitably find too broad or too restrictive. We choose not to analyze pornography "as something that exists outside" of the competing discourses that attempt to persuade political audiences as to "the correct, appropriate, or preferred representation" of reality (Elmer 1988, p. 46; Mehan & Wills 1988, p. 364). We recognize that each competing perspective or ideological position on pornography attempts to construct "clarity out of ambiguity" (Mehan & Wills 1988, p. 364). Each has its own "restrictive logic" that is related to the particular *epistemological* and *ontological* assumptions in which it is grounded (Baudrillard 1981, p. 92).[7]

We believe that the pornography debate has proceeded without careful articulation of these assumptions, and hence the most crucial elements of each ideological position have often remained taken for granted and absent from the discussion. The discourse of each perspective is distinct for what it reveals as well as for what it conceals (Elmer 1988). In other words, each attempts to establish particular claims about pornography and the centrality of certain relevant issues, while deemphasizing other claims and the significance of other issues. Each attempts to fill the "hole in the theory" by addressing the issues the others neglect (p. 48). This inevitably leads representatives of the different positions to miscommunicate or "talk past each other," arguing about issues the other does not fully appreciate or comprehend. We believe, however, that it is only through dialogue that any meaningful resolution of the debate can take place, for the significance of pornography may lie somewhere *between* rather than *within* each of the competing perspectives (see Holquist 1983; Mehan & Wills 1988).

NOTES

1. Arguments in favor and against the civil rights approach will be discussed in Chapter 7.

2. Among men sympathetic to feminism, arguments have generally mirrored the feminist antipornography/anticensorship debate regarding

the harm of pornography and appropriate legal strategies (see *Changing Men* 1985; Kimmel 1990).

3. Although it is most common to refer to nineteenth-century activism as the "first wave of feminism" and the contemporary movement as the "second wave," some scholars distinguish the wave of feminism that grew out of the abolitionist struggles of the 1830s from the wave which became focused on women's suffrage that developed from the progressive reform era of the 1890s (Taylor 1983).

4. The Contagious Disease Acts in Great Britain required that prostitutes register with police and undergo biweekly examinations of venereal disease. Since the Contagious Disease Acts also authorized police to detain for examination any woman suspected of prostitution, they not only regulated and controlled prostitutes, but served to limit the mobility and freedom of all women. For further discussion of prostitution in Great Britain and of Josephine Butler's campaign against the Contagious Disease Acts implemented in the 1860s, see Barry (1979) and Walkowitz (1980).

5. In 1873 the U.S. Congress passed the Comstock Act, which prohibited the mailing of obscene materials. Anthony Comstock was the founder of the New York Society for the Suppression of Vice (Downs 1989).

6. Some analysts distinguish ideology from other cultural forms such as "common sense," viewing ideology as one phase in the development of culture (Swidler 1986). In this view, ideology "is a highly articulated, self-conscious belief and ritual system, aspiring to offer a unified answer to problems of social action . . . that does not 'come naturally' " (pp. 279, 284). In contrast, common sense "is the set of assumptions so unselfconscious as to seem a natural, transparent, undeniable part of the structure of the world" (p. 279; see Geertz 1975).

7. Epistemology refers to the particular theory of knowledge assumed by the different positions; it deals with the origins, methods, limits, and validity of knowledge—how one "knows" what is "true." Ontology refers to the study of being, the nature of reality, or the essence of things; it deals with questions of human nature and the fundamental principles assumed to underlie society, sexuality, and psychological processes.

2

Traditional Perspectives on Pornography: Popular Positions and Governmental Commissions

The competing feminist perspectives on pornography are concerned with the significance of pornography for women and female sexuality. Issues of gender, however, are generally absent or excluded from the traditional discourses on pornography. In this chapter, we place the feminist debate in broader perspective by examining traditional positions on pornography as they are embodied in popular opinion and in governmental commissions in the United States.[1] In the first section we contrast religious-conservative and civil libertarian positions. In the second section we contrast the 1970 Commission on Obscenity and Pornography and the 1986 Attorney General's Commission on Pornography (Meese Commission) and consider feminist critiques of their procedures and results.[2]

POPULAR POSITIONS ON PORNOGRAPHY

Religious-Conservative

The traditional conservative antipornography position has its roots in a religious ideology that restricts sex to heterosexual marriage. Although some fundamentalists deny the legitimacy of sex for pleasure and regret that sex has become separated from its "God-given goal," that is, procreation (Osanka & Johann 1989, p. 258), contemporary adherents often approve of nonprocreative sex in the context of marriage (Cottle et al. 1989; Weaver 1989). Barbara Ehrenreich, Elizabeth Hess, and Gloria Jacobs (1986) observe that the sexual revolution has, to some extent, "penetrated even the self-enclosed world of right-wing fundamentalism," and that sex books and manuals for Christian audiences have become increasingly popular (p. 135; see LaHaye & LaHaye 1976; Morgan 1973).

The religious-conservative opposition to pornography assumes that people possess an inherent human propensity to sin and that pornography undermines the family, traditional authority, and moral fabric of society (Cottle et al. 1989; Minnery 1986; Osanka & Johann 1989; Wood & Hughes 1984). Pornography is seen as unleashing undesirable libidinal impulses, luring people down a morally corrupt path of premarital sexuality, sexual promiscuity, adultery, perversity, and "abnormal" sexual behavior (including homosexuality). In short, religious-conservatives believe that pornography is a sin and an offense against God and that it "denies the image of God within us" (Cottle et al. 1989; Osanka & Johann 1989, p. 260). Thus, they feel that each of us is "his brother's keeper" and that "we do no one a service by taking the attitude that what others do is their own concern and not that of their neighbor" (Cottle et al. 1989, p. 313).

Central to the religious-conservative position is the danger pornography is believed to pose to the healthy moral development of children. Religious-conservatives believe that pornography teaches young people that sex is just a physical act rather than an integral part of a meaningful emotional relationship. They fear that pornography will lead young people to experiment with premarital sex and thus increase the rate of teenage pregnancy and promiscuity (Cottle et al. 1989).

Religious-conservatives also believe that pornography is addictive—that its users become habituated and desensitized. What may have been shocking at one time becomes commonplace, and the pain and the degradation of others in pornography become trivial matters (Cottle et al. 1989; Minnery 1986).

In addition, religious-conservatives have adopted some of the discourse of the feminist antipornography position. They believe that pornography promotes or encourages rape and other forms of sexual violence and that both children and adults are often forced into making pornographic films against their will. Thus, they do not believe that the U.S. Constitution should be used to "protect the rights of pornographers who encourage the exploitation and dehumanization" of others, and they favor enforcement of criminal laws against the production and distribution of pornography (Cottle et al. 1989, p. 314).

While religious-conservatives share with antipornography feminists a concern about the harm of pornography and the dangers of untrammeled individual freedom (see Clark 1983; MacKinnon 1984), they disagree about how pornography actually affects male consumers.[3] Antipornography feminists have been concerned that pornography socializes or conditions men to believe that women are sexually insatiable, desirous of male dominance, and even masochistic. Religious conservatives, in contrast, do not believe that pornography teaches men that what they read or see in magazines and films accurately reflects "what women are really like" (Cottle et al. 1989, p. 320). They are more concerned that pornography promotes sexual obsession and perversity and tempts men to have illicit sex. Moreover, since antipornography feminists accept the legitimacy of nonmarital sex and homosexuality, they do not rule out some varieties of sexual experience that religious-conservatives condemn. They also do not object to certain sex education materials or erotic imagery (for example, sexually explicit materials that involve depictions of consensual, nonexploitive relations) that religious-conservatives might want to censor, and, of course, they disagree about a wide range of other social issues such as abortion and the ERA. In fact, feminists argue that traditional religious views of the divine as superior and dominant and of humanity as inferior and submissive have served to justify women's oppression. As Mary Jo Weaver (1989) observes, "This revealed order of things, as found in the Bible and in the Christian tradition, is presumed to be replicated in human relations so that the male inherits the lordly qualities of God the Father, while the female is enjoined to be submissive to God's rule as it is enacted by the male (father, husband, brother, bishop)" (p. 70). Moreover, anthropological research indicates that rape is more common in cultures that worship a male creator or deity as opposed to a female creator or deity (Sanday 1981).[4]

Civil Libertarian

The contemporary antipornography movement, consisting primarily of feminists and religious-conservatives, has brought forth the traditional opposition to censorship from liberals and libertarians. Liberalism and libertarianism are by no means identical political philosophies. Contemporary liberals generally support an activist state to promote social equality and civil rights and to mitigate the adverse effects of an unregulated market economy. Libertarians, reflecting the liberalism prior to the "New Deal" of the 1930s, generally advocate a minimalist (noninterventionist) conception of the state. Whereas liberals often divorce questions of individual freedom from economic issues, libertarians believe it is impossible to simultaneously interfere with the economy and maintain individual freedom. Although liberals and libertarians diverge on questions of economics, egalitarianism, and the role of government in society, both endorse a civil libertarian approach to pornography that emphasizes the inviolability of individual rights and the sanctity of individual freedom.

According to the civil libertarian view, central to the pornography debate is the issue of freedom, that is, freedom from state censorship and state invasion of privacy. Civil libertarians strongly oppose all forms of censorship and assert that First Amendment freedoms of speech and press must be preserved. They believe a free society must be willing to tolerate cultural products that offend some people (Cottle et al. 1989; Emerson 1985; Lynn &

Goldstein 1985; Osanka & Johann 1989; Sheinfeld 1985).

Many who adopt the civil libertarian position believe it is impossible to arrive at a definition of pornography with which everyone will agree. Definitions of pornography, they claim, are influenced by individual tastes and preferences, and what one person finds unappealing or even offensive, another might find artistic or erotic. This viewpoint employs a "slippery slope" argument, asserting that attempts to censor "hard-core" pornography will lead inevitably to the banning of magazines like *Playboy* and *Penthouse* (which some believe contain "good articles" and beautiful nudes that are "tastefully photographed") and to a suppression of erotic imagery in all media (Cottle et al. 1989, p. 317). Besides, civil libertarians generally believe that censorship would be ineffective because pornography would "just go underground" (p. 318).

Many civil libertarians (particularly contemporary liberals) often dismiss antipornography sentiments as sexual prudery and criticize antipornography adherents for having a "moralistic" and "self-righteous wisdom" and for attempting to decide for others what they should see and read (p. 317). They view human sexuality as naturally good, a feature of existence to be enjoyed, and are more concerned about the harm of sexual repression than about the harm of pornography. Many feel that we should be "more open and relaxed about nudity and sexuality," believe that "we're overdoing it with all this concern about pornography," and fear that "we're going back to the days of the Puritan ethic." These civil libertarians are not persuaded that any substantial evidence exists that pornography is harmful, at least to adults. They find some types of pornography erotic and appealing, especially now that it can be watched on cable TV and/or a VCR "in the privacy of their own homes." Although they admit that pornography can become boring after one's initial curiosity is satisfied, they feel that some pornography may have beneficial effects—that is, it may reduce sexual inhibitions, increase willingness to try new sexual experiences, and improve couples' sexual relationships. Furthermore, some resent having to defend their enjoyment of pornography, believing that "sexual arousal is its own best self-defense."

In sum, the civil libertarian position invokes the First Amendment freedoms of speech and press as inalienable rights essential to the preservation of a free society. Thus even if definitional problems associated with pornography could be resolved, and the "slippery slope" argument were invalid, censorship would still be wrong. But in spite of their principled opposition to censorship, many civil libertarians are not necessarily First Amendment absolutists. For instance, many express a respect for the types of regulation allowed by the U.S. Supreme Court, are generally comfortable with the *Miller v. California* (1973) decision that allows communities to enforce their own standards regarding pornography, and believe that the "majority should decide if pornography should be available" (Cottle et al. 1989, p. 318; see Chapter 7). They also agree with the *New York v. Ferber* (1982) decision that allows the prohibition of child pornography and believe that "society must take steps to prevent children from being exposed" (Cottle et al. 1989, p. 318). This protective stance toward children suggests an underlying concern that pornography may have some harmful effects. With regard to adult pornography, however, this concern for harm is absent or it does not override their First Amendment priorities or their desire to have access to pornography. If there *are* risks involved, civil libertarians assume adults have the maturity to make responsible decisions for themselves. They are thus willing to allow the marketplace to regulate the supply and demand of cultural products associated with sexuality.

U.S. GOVERNMENTAL COMMISSIONS

1970 Commission on Obscenity and Pornography

In 1967 President Lyndon Johnson established the Commission on Obscenity and Pornography (report published in 1970) to investigate "a matter of national concern" (Hawkins & Zimring

1988, p. 7).[5] Representatives from the areas of law, social science, religion, broadcasting, and publishing were appointed to the commission. The commission was organized into panels working on four topics: effects, traffic and distribution, legal issues, and positive approaches. In spite of its title, the commission avoided using the terms "obscenity" and "pornography," due to their legalistic or derogatory connotations, preferring to use instead the terms "explicit sexual material," "sexually oriented material," or "erotica" to refer to the subject matter under investigation. After the commissioners reviewed available research as well as the results of new studies they had commissioned, the commission concluded (1) that there was no empirical evidence that such materials played any role in causing sex crimes or other criminal behavior, (2) that established patterns of sexual behavior were not altered by exposure to such materials, and (3) that fears about negative effects were unwarranted.

In the 1970s feminists appeared to be in agreement about the inadequacies of the 1970 commission. Feminists who are today identified with both the antipornography camp (for example, Bart & Jozsa 1980) and the anticensorship camp (for example, McCormack 1978) criticized the commission. Feminists criticized the commission for its failure to distinguish different types of sexually explicit materials (for example, erotica, violent pornography, sex education literature) and for relying on empirical studies that also failed to make such distinctions and that contained other methodological deficiencies—for example, reliance on one-time exposure to pornography (Bart & Jozsa 1980; Einsiedel 1989). In addition, the commission relied on flawed retrospective studies which defined "sex offenders" as a broad category that included homosexuals and exhibitionists as well as rapists (who were only a minority of the sample) (Diamond 1980). From these studies, which suggested that "sex offenders" actually had less exposure to pornography during adolescence than other adults, the commission concluded that there was no evidence of a link between pornography and rape. Furthermore, the commission's deliberations were conducted when violent or aggressive pornography was relatively rare, and thus the studies utilized did not generally include stimuli that involved rape or other forms of coercive sexuality (Donnerstein et al. 1987; Malamuth 1985). In light of their concerns about violence against women, feminists were particularly critical of the studies which claimed that pornography had a cathartic effect (that is, it inhibited aggressive behavior) (Einsiedel 1989) and of the commission's conclusion that pornography was "essentially a medium for sexual expression" that fostered "more agreeable and increased openness in marital communication" (Diamond 1980, pp. 687, 691).[6]

Although the commission favored legislation that would prohibit "open public displays of sexually explicit pictorial materials" as well as the sale and distribution of such materials to young people (Hawkins & Zimring 1988, pp. 139–40), it recommended the repeal of antipornography legislation involving adults and expressed a concern that censorship threatened the foundation of American liberties. Feminists noted the discrepancy between this stance and that of the 1969 National Commission on the Causes and Prevention of Violence, which was more receptive to some censorship of violence (Diamond 1980). The "double standard" toward censorship represented by the two commissions was attributed to the commission on obscenity's failure to recognize the violence in pornography. It was also attributed to an attitudinal complex in which "macho" pride in sexual virility led the commission on obscenity to appreciate pornography, while anxiety about male sexual identity induced the commission on violence to disapprove of male-against-male violent films (McCormack 1978).

The 1970 Commission on Obscenity and Pornography appeared to endorse and legitimize the civil libertarian view of pornography. However, following the release of the commission's report, the U.S. Senate passed a resolution condemning it, and President Richard Nixon warned that "an attitude of permissiveness . . . regarding pornography . . . would contribute to an atmosphere condoning anarchy . . . [and threaten] our social order [and] moral principles" (Kendrick 1987, p. 219; Hawkins & Zimring 1988).

The Meese Commission

In 1985 President Ronald Reagan established the Attorney General's Commission on Pornography (1986), headed by Edwin Meese, to "officially" overturn the earlier report and spearhead a national effort to increase enforcement of antipornography laws. The official charter of the Meese Commission was to find "more effective ways in which the spread of pornography could be constrained" (Hawkins & Zimring 1988, p. 113). The members of the commission included persons with backgrounds in law, behavioral medicine and psychiatry, broadcasting and publishing, and market research. Also included on the commission were representatives of the religious-based opposition to pornography: a legal counsel for Citizens for Decency through Law, a leader of the fundamentalist organization Focus on the Family, and a Franciscan priest. The chair of the commission was an antipornography prosecutor who was "praised by President Reagan for closing down every adult bookstore in his district" (Vance 1986, p. 76).

For a year the commission held hearings around the country on preselected topics related to pornography—that is, production and distribution, law enforcement, organized crime, social science findings, and child pornography. However, it neglected feminist topics such as pornography and domestic violence, pornography and the status of women, and pornography and female sexual freedom (Van Gelder 1986). The overwhelming majority of witnesses supported increased restrictions on, if not total elimination of, sexually explicit materials. Law enforcement and anti-vice officers were heavily represented as witnesses, as were spokespersons for conservative antipornography groups such as Citizens for Decency through Law. Civil libertarians (for example, the American Civil Liberties Union) and feminists (for example, Dworkin, MacKinnon, and the members of FACT) were given an opportunity to testify, although they had little impact on the commission's findings and recommendations (Douglas 1986; Vance 1986). Virtually every claim made by antipornography witnesses was accepted with little probing or only cursory requests for evidence, while witnesses who did not favor the commission's agenda were often treated with rudeness, hostility, and criticism (Van Gelder 1986; Vance 1986).

Although the traditional religious-conservative view undoubtedly underlay the position of some members, the commission's antipornography position was "modernized" by drawing on social science and feminist discourse (Vance 1986). The harm of pornography was said to be violence, not sin or immorality, and the evidence for such harm came from a controversial interpretation of the social science research on pornography (see Chapter 6). The commission's interpretation of this literature was immediately criticized by some of the leading researchers in the field (Donnerstein & Linz 1986a). The commission was also critiqued for its faulty use of public opinion data (Smith 1987).

The testimonies of Linda Marchiano, Dottie Meyer, and Andrea Dworkin at the New York hearings, as well as the response of the commission to these women, offer considerable insight into the underlying assumptions of the commission (Van Gelder 1986). Marchiano, formerly billed as Linda Lovelace in the film *Deep Throat*, was one of several victims of pornography who testified about sexual coercion and moral decadence in the pornography industry. Particularly noteworthy was Marchiano's account of how pornography had harmed her relationship with her children and affected her ability to teach them proper moral values (see Lovelace & McGrady 1980). On the other hand, Meyer, a *Penthouse* executive and former centerfold model, testified that she was "*not* a victim of so-called pornography" and that she had had "a traditional upbringing" and a happy seventeen-year marriage. "I'm a typical suburbanite. I cook and I clean my own home and I even take out the garbage." In spite of their differing opinions about pornography, Marchiano and Meyer both seemed to be traditionally feminine women who understood their "experiences in the context of marriage-centered womanhood" and their ability to carry out their feminine roles (Van Gelder 1986, p. 54).

In contrast, Dworkin, "*the* official feminist presence at the [New York] hearings" (p. 54), was not well received, and she was criticized by the commission for concentrating her remarks on the victimization of women and for neglecting pornography involving children, men, and homosexuals. It appeared that some members of the commission were responding to Dworkin's refusal to address the issues, as had Marchiano and Meyer, "in terms of its impact on 'family' or 'marriage' or some other approved institution." Dworkin was also criticized by the anticensorship coalition consisting of FACT, the ACLU, *Penthouse*, and professional groups of librarians, writers, and artists. They viewed Dworkin as a "turncoat" and a "renegade feminist" (p. 54; Hertzberg 1986, p. 23). Because she had a history of involvement with leftist politics and her arguments were grounded in feminist theory, she challenged anticensorship forces intellectually in a way that right-wing moralists did not. At the same time, one of Dworkin's colleagues criticized a *Ms.* magazine writer for even interviewing FACT members, since, as she said, "they couldn't possibly be feminists" (Van Gelder 1986, p. 54).

Although the commission was unable to agree on a definition of pornography, it identified four categories of sexual imagery: (1) violent pornography, (2) degrading (nonviolent) pornography (for example, oral, anal, group, masturbatory, and homosexual sex), (3) nonviolent and nondegrading sexually explicit materials (for example, depictions of sexual intercourse), and (4) simple nudity. The commission concluded that the first two categories were definitely harmful. One member of the commission, following some radical feminists, incorporated into the "degrading" category material that depicted people as existing solely for the sexual satisfaction of others or in subordinate roles in sexual relations. More moderate commission members wanted to define the latter two categories as harmless, but more conservative members thought that any sexually explicit material was harmful if it provoked people to engage in illicit (that is, nonmarital) sex (Douglas 1986; Hertzberg 1986; Vance 1986).

The commission recommended both increased enforcement of

existing obscenity laws and the passage of new laws (Douglas 1986; Vance 1986). While the commission endorsed strategies against pornography advocated by some feminists, such as boycotts of stores that sell pornographic materials (see Lederer 1980) and laws providing civil remedies for women harmed by pornography, many feminists expressed concern that the commission's recommendations would be used to repress sex education materials (for example, the book *Our Bodies, Ourselves*) as well as nonviolent, nondegrading erotic imagery (Rich 1985; Vance 1986). In addition, the commission only reluctantly supported programs to educate children about sexual abuse, for it was concerned that these programs would be perceived as an endorsement of sex education or that they would encourage children to make false accusations. Furthermore, it did not support the decriminalization of laws against female workers in the sex industry (for example, prostitutes, pornography models), preferring instead to increase arrests of these women (Vance 1986).

Thus, anticensorship feminists concluded that the Meese Commission's recommendations constituted "a major defeat" for feminism (p. 80). Viewing the commission in the context of the Reagan administration's antifeminist political agenda, these feminists argued that the only thing women could expect from the commission would be "a hit list with masturbation and sodomy on it" (Ann Snitow, quoted in Van Gelder 1986, p. 83). On the other hand, some antipornography feminists commended the commission "for being the first federal government body to report on the systematic campaign of abuse, terror, and discrimination . . . against [women]" (Dorchen Leidholdt, founder of Women Against Pornography, quoted in Douglas 1986, p. 4).

CONCLUSION

The Meese Commission and the 1970 commission lent credibility to the religious-conservative and civil libertarian positions, respectively. Religious-conservatives, like antipornography feminists, believe that sexuality is an appropriate concern for the public agenda. They desire public control over pornography to protect people from what they perceive as its harmful consequences and support state-sponsored efforts to censor and criminalize at least some forms of pornography. However, the significant differences between religious-conservatives and antipornography feminists make any political coalition tenuous and conflictual. By promoting antipornography politics, feminists face the danger of facilitating religious-conservatives' broader antifeminist agenda.

Liberals and libertarians view sexuality as a private experience that is generally separate from any appropriate sphere of public control. Although they often express concerns about child pornography and about pornography's effects on children, many (but not all) reject antipornography arguments concerning the harm pornography may do to adults. They support a civil liberties approach that allows individuals the right to choose and have access to pornography. Anticensorship feminists share much common ground with traditional civil libertarians. However, an alignment of these forces minimizes women's particular vulnerability to sexual victimization.

Whereas anticensorship forces found support in the findings and recommendations of the 1970 commission, antipornography forces found support in the Meese Commission. However, both of these state-sponsored inquiries were significantly influenced by ideological preferences and political considerations. Gordon Hawkins and Frank Zimring (1988) view both commissions' deliberations as "ceremonies of adjustment to the social fact of [pornography's] widespread availability" and believe that the Meese Commission was more a "symbolic denunciation" of the 1970s commission than a serious effort to change the status quo (pp. xi, 225). On the other hand, both antipornography and anticensorship feminists want to change the status quo, although they disagree about the direction of such a change.

NOTES

1. Traditional perspectives as embodied in U.S. Supreme Court obscenity decisions will be discussed in Chapter 7. For discussions of the 1979 Home Office Departmental Committee on Obscenity and Film Censorship (Williams Committee) in Great Britain and the 1985 Special Committee on Pornography and Prostitution (Fraser Committee) in Canada, see Hawkins and Zimring (1988) and Franklin Mark Osanka and Sara Lee Johann (1989).

2. Much of the discussion of the religious-conservative and civil libertarian positions is based on an empirical study conducted by the authors (Cottle et al. 1989). Using Q-methodology, respondents sorted a sample of eighty-six opinion statements on definitions of pornography, personal reactions to pornography, pornography's causes and effects, and social policy recommendations. Factor analysis was used to identify clusters of individuals who shared common subjectively defined points of view on pornography. The dominant patterns of response that emerged from the analysis correspond to those we have labeled religious-conservative, civil libertarian, and antipornography feminist. Parts of this section were adapted from Charles Cottle, Patricia Searles, Ronald Berger, and Beth Ann Pierce (1989) and Ronald J. Berger, Patricia Searles, and Charles E. Cottle (1990b).

3. In comparison to religious-conservatives, antipornography feminists tend to be young, single, childless, highly educated, and middle class (Cottle et al. 1989; Kirkpatrick & Zurcher 1983).

4. Herman (1988) also notes "the frequent presence of extreme religious fundamentalism and rigidly punitive sexual attitudes in the backgrounds of sex offenders" (p. 711).

5. Parts of this section on U.S. governmental commissions were adapted from Berger et al. (1990a, 1990b).

6. Some feminists are more sympathetic to the view that pornography has a cathartic effect (McCormack 1985b).

3

Pornography and the Feminist Sexuality Debate: Radical and Libertarian Feminism

As we have seen, issues of gender are generally absent or excluded from the traditional antipornography and anticensorship positions that continue to dominate popular opinion and political debate.[1] By introducing gender into the contemporary discourse, feminism challenges these perspectives. Nevertheless, both antipornography and anticensorship feminists have found themselves in precarious political alliances with nonfeminist forces—antipornography feminists with religious-conservatives and anticensorship feminists with civil libertarians, neither of which are necessarily supportive of broader feminist goals. Clearly, the traditional "left-right" political continuum is insufficient to characterize the different sides of the pornography debate.

The feminist debate has polarized around the confrontation between radical and libertarian feminists. Although both sides share a critique of patriarchal institutions and values, they articulate divergent views regarding the problem of violence against women and the nature of sexuality and its representation. In the 1970s, both sides called for reproductive rights for women (for example, the right to abortion). They also called for a general cultural change regarding female sexuality, asserting women's "right" to experience sexual pleasure (for example, orgasms, nonmarital sex, lesbian sex). These objectives were bolstered by the U.S. Supreme Court "pro-choice" abortion decision of *Roe v. Wade* (1973) and by the works of sexuality researchers who offered frank information about women's orgasmic capacities and sexual preferences (Barbach 1976; Friday 1974; Hite 1976; Masters & Johnson 1966; see Ehrenreich et al. 1986).

By the late 1970s, the unity among feminists had begun to fade in response to the growing attack against misogynist media imagery. Actually, feminist concern with media imagery had begun some years before the split in the movement occurred. For instance, in 1966 the statement of purpose of the National Organization for Women (NOW) asserted that "we will protest, and endeavor to change, the false image of women now prevalent in the main media" (quoted in Ellis et al. 1986, p. 26). In 1968 a New York group called Radical Women protested the Miss America pageant, passing out leaflets which claimed that "Miss America and *Playboy*'s centerfold are sisters under the skin. To win approval, we must be both sexy and wholesome. . . . Deviation of any sort brings, we are told, disaster: 'You won't get a man!' " (p. 26).

In the following years, a number of demonstrations were held around the country that called attention to various aspects of sexist media representation. For example, in 1976 members of Women Against Violence Against Women (WAVAW) defaced a Los Angeles billboard advertisement for the Rolling Stones that depicted a woman in chains with bruises on her legs and face and a caption that read: "I'm black and blue from the Rolling Stones and I love it." A demonstration was staged that received national press coverage and forced Warner Brothers to remove the ad. That same year a conference on "Violence Against Women" held in San Francisco resulted in the formation of an activist organization, Women Against Violence in Pornography and Media (WAVPM). The following year women in several cities protested the showing of *Snuff*, a film that was billed as containing footage of a woman who was actually "tortured, mutilated, and murdered for sexual stimulation," and the first antirape "Take Back the Night March" was held in Pittsburgh to "dramatize women's insistence on the right to enjoy public space in safety" (Lederer 1980, p. 15; Ellis et al. 1986, p. 27). In 1978 WAVPM organized a conference on "Feminist Perspectives on Pornography" that included a march by 5,000 women through the pornography district in San Francisco.

Evidence of disunity surfaced, however, when in 1979 a lesbian sadomasochism (S & M) group in San Francisco called Samois held a public forum challenging WAVPM's depiction of lesbian S & M as violence against women. In that and the following year, several articles by feminists appeared which criticized the antipornography feminist analysis of pornography (Ellis et al. 1986). By 1982 it was apparent that a serious difference of opinion existed among feminists when a conference on sexuality was held at Barnard College of Columbia University on the theme of "pleasure and danger" (Vance 1984). A group of antipornography feminists reacted by staging a protest "against S & M" and criticized the conference for promoting "antifeminist sexuality."

The two sides of the feminist pornography debate began to crystallize around the *radical* and *libertarian* feminist positions. Whereas the former focused on those aspects of sexuality that victimized and oppressed women, the latter focused on ways women could overcome sexual repression and achieve sexual liberation. Radical feminists emphasized issues of rape, battering, and pornography. They developed an analysis of violence against women, which they associated with male dominance, male-centered sex, and compulsory heterosexuality (Barry 1979; Dworkin & MacKinnon 1988; Lederer 1980). While they were supportive of homosexuality, they were critical of sadomasochism, including lesbian S & M, for perpetuating sexual norms of domination and submission (Linden et al. 1982). On the other hand, libertarian feminists questioned what they perceived to be radical feminists' tendency to conflate sex and violence and advocate a moralistic vision of "politically correct" relationships and "vanilla sex" (Ellis et al. 1986; Rubin et al. 1981; Vance & Snitow 1984). They accepted lesbian S & M, arguing that the masochist remains in control and that the participants role-play and experiment with dominant and submissive positions (Ehrenreich et al. 1986; Williams 1989a).

As feminist writings proliferated, other perspectives began to take shape. In addition to radical feminism, liberal, Marxist, and socialist feminism became identified as the major theoretical perspectives offering comprehensive philosophical and political points of view about gender and society (Jaggar 1983; Messer-schmidt 1986).[2] Libertarian feminism, in contrast, remained more narrowly focused on issues pertaining to sexuality. In this chapter we consider the radical and libertarian positions on pornography and their underlying assumptions. In the following chapter we broaden the discussion by evaluating the implications of other feminist perspectives that have not yet been as central to the pornography debate, including black feminism, which has been offered as a distinct feminist viewpoint (Collins 1986).

RADICAL FEMINISM

While it is difficult to identify a single radical feminist analysis of women's oppression in general and pornography in particular (Jaggar 1983), the epistemology underlying radical feminism assumes that all knowledge is political and rooted in subjective human experience. Thus, radical feminism makes "no pretence of detached impartiality" or objectivity (p. 369). It views traditional *positivist* methods of acquiring scientific knowledge as adopting a "masculine standpoint" that posits a dualism or separation between the observer and the observed and between rationality and feeling (Stacey & Thorne 1985). In contrast, radical feminism adopts "women's standpoint" as the basis for acquiring reliable knowledge, and emphasizes strategies such as consciousness-raising sessions, whereby the personal experiences of women are translated into the power to identify, name, and overcome oppressive social conditions (Jaggar 1983; MacKinnon 1979; Smith 1979). In contrast to positivist epistemology, radical feminists include feelings and emotions as avenues of understanding social reality, and they have provided much insight into women's experience of pain and anger in relation to sexuality.

The social theory of radical feminism asserts that the "social relations of the sexes are organized so men may dominate and women must submit," and it holds that "the primary social sphere of male power" resides in the area of sexuality (Bart 1989, p. 539; MacKinnon 1982, p. 15). Radical feminists believe that male-dominated or patriarchal societies are hierarchically organized to expropriate women's sexuality (including their procreative capacities) for the use of males, and that sexuality for women thus involves risks and abusive practices. Violence against women is maintained by the institutionalization of a dichotomy between dominant masculine roles and subordinate feminine roles in the patriarchal family and by sexual scripts that promote sexual coercion as normal behavior and as a source of sexual pleasure for men and women (Barry 1979; Jackson 1978). Under conditions of gender inequality, male dominance is normative and even eroticized, rendering the notion of "consent" to sexual interaction problematic (Berger et al. 1986; MacKinnon 1983). According to Susan Griffin (1981), "In our culture male eroticism is wedded to power. Not only should a man be taller and stronger than a female in the perfect love-match, but he must also demonstrate his superior strength in gestures of dominance which are perceived as amorous" (p. 78).

Traditional gender roles include sexual scripts that involve an active male and a passive female (Jackson 1978; Weis & Borges 1973). Men and women are socialized to expect males to initiate sexual encounters and "seduce" their sexual partners. According to the scripts, men and women expect females to put up some resistance that may not be indicative of their true feelings and desires. Thus men often believe that "women mean 'yes' when they say 'no'," and that too hasty acceptance of women's protestations would deprive them of sexual experiences they could attain with more persistence (Clark & Lewis 1977). The scripts include culturally available "rape myths" involving the belief that women are tempting seductresses who invite sexual encounters, that women secretly want to be raped, that women eventually relax and enjoy rape, and that men have urgent sexual needs which prevent them from controlling their behavior (Berger et al. 1986; Burt 1980). They allow men to interpret their use of force in sexual interaction as a legitimate strategy, to lessen their sense of responsibility, and to deny that inappropriate coercion has occurred (Scully & Marolla 1984).[3] Under these conditions, women may perceive no alternative but to acquiesce and may prefer acquiescence to the "risk of physical injury or humiliation of a lost fight" (MacKinnon 1983, p. 650). Some women may even learn to eroticize dominance. In either case, genuine consent (a freely given agreement between persons of equal power and rationality) is absent from many sexual encounters.[4]

According to radical feminists, genuine consent is absent as well from much of women's exposure to pornography (Bart et al. 1985; MacKinnon 1986). They argue that pornographic imagery is pervasive in the environment, and that women are often confronted with it in the home, in stores, and in the workplace. Women may also feel compelled, pressured, or forced to watch pornographic films and videos, to pose for home photographs, to perform before a video camera, or to replicate acts depicted in pornography in order to please their partners, not appear prudish, or avoid verbal or physical abuse.[5] In addition, forced exposure to pornography also accompanies much incest and child abuse (Champion 1986; Osanka & Johann 1989).

In contrast to the hierarchical and dichotomous gender relations of patriarchy and its prescribed patterns of sexual interaction, radical feminists have attempted to develop a vision and practice of egalitarian social relationships, particularly in the area of sexuality (Jaggar 1983). According to radical feminists, traditional male-dominated sexuality endorses an atomistic ontology that involves dominance, manipulation, and performance, that separates sex and affection, and that emphasizes the genital and visual aspects of sexuality. In contrast, they envision a sexuality that is holistic, that is, one expressing love, emotional intimacy, and tenderness between equal and consenting partners (Cohen 1986; Ferguson 1984; Jaggar 1983).

Radical feminists emphasize the harm of pornography to *women*, in contrast to the traditional (nonfeminist) antipornography view that emphasizes the harm of pornography to the family and moral fabric of society. Andrea Dworkin (1981) and Catharine MacKinnon (1986, 1984) articulate an analysis of pornography that places it "at the center of a cycle of abuse" and that views it as a "core constitutive practice" that helps to institutionalize and legitimize gender inequality (1986, p. 47; 1984, p. 27). Radical feminists assert that pornography is both a form of misogyny and coercive sexuality and a system of sexual exploitation and female sexual slavery, which also involves rape, incest, prostitution, and battering (Barry 1979).[6] It is a method of socialization that causes and perpetuates acts of violence against women, creates a social climate in which sexual assault and abuse are tolerated, and objectifies, dehumanizes, and degrades women (Clark 1983; Lederer 1980). Moreover, pornography makes gender inequality appear "sexy" and "natural," and it constitutes the very meaning of sexuality by eroticizing dominance and submission in sexual relationships and by conditioning men's sexual response to the powerlessness of women (Bart 1989). Pornography constructs *who women are* since "men's power over women means that the way men see women defines who women can be" (MacKinnon 1984, p. 326).

Pornography, from this perspective, is not mere fantasy or simulation. It is not a distortion or "artificial overlay upon an unalterable substratum of essential sexual being," but it is sexual reality itself (MacKinnon 1984, p. 326; see Dworkin 1981). Pornography is not an "idea" any more than racial segregation is an "idea." Like segregation, it is a concrete, discriminatory social practice that institutionalizes the inferiority and subordination of one group to another. Hence, radical feminists favor legal remedies such as the antipornography civil rights ordinance that would enable women to redress this discrimination.

According to Kathleen Barry's (1979) radical feminist analysis, pornography is the embodiment of "cultural sadism"—that ideology which depicts sexual violence as normative and pleasurable for women. By editing out "women's pain" (p. 209), pornography disguises the inequality and coercion inherent in its creation and fuses male aggression with romantic love. Pornography is a principal medium through which cultural sadism is diffused into the mainstream culture and integrated into the sexual practices of individuals.

Barry develops a radical feminist ontology of pornography and its relationship to sexual fantasy, arguing that pornography is intended for its effect—that is, to elicit sexual response in viewers. The pornographic experience is stored in the memory and is retrievable to fantasy and action. Although consumers of pornography have some choice over what to interpret as reality, what to attribute to fantasy or distortion, and what to act out, their choices are based on those experiences that have produced the greatest sexual stimulation and that therefore have received the most reinforcement. While "fantasy in and of itself is neither positive nor negative behavior" (p. 211), it is often the link between one's self and one's sexual life. Consequently, personal fantasy, highly susceptible to pornography, may enter into sexual interaction with others. The "social-sexual reality" of the other person is objectified and replaced by the fantasy, reducing the need for people to relate to each other as subjects (p. 213). As MacKinnon (1984) writes, "men *have sex* with their *image* of a woman" (p. 328).

Furthermore, when pornographic fantasies are violent, sexual arousal becomes conditioned to violence and internal prohibitions against acting out such fantasies are reduced (Malamuth 1985). Cheryl Champion (1986) estimates that about 40 percent of clinical sex offender cases involve perpetrators who use pornography, typically in a very compulsive and obsessive manner. These offenders "have an active fantasy life involving the use of pornographic materials for masturbation, fantasy contemplation, and actual acting out of their scenarios on their victims" (p. 24). Judith Herman (1988), noting the large number of sex offenders who commit their first offense during adolescence, suggests that pornography may contribute to consolidating violent sexual fantasies during young males' formative years.

Susanne Kappeler (1986) offers another variant of the radical feminist position. Like Dworkin and MacKinnon, she sees an interrelationship between "representational practices which construct sexuality and actual sexual practices" (p. 2). She argues that the fantasy-reality distinction is a false dichotomy since representations "have a continued existence in reality as objects of exchange" (p. 3). Moreover, Kappeler sees no meaningful difference between pornography and erotica, attributing any perceived distinction to that which exists between "art" and "bad taste mass culture," or between "vaginas represented by men and vaginas represented by women" (p. 40). Consequently, she does not "believe in the possibility (or desirability) of laying down a programme of 'feminist aesthetics', a charter of ideologically 'correct' procedures, a catalogue of 'positive images' " (p. 220). Contrary to the views of libertarian feminists (see below), the situation cannot be remedied "by appointing more women pornographers." The objectification of others characterized in the imagery of both male- and female-produced pornography remains the same. Through both the production and consumption of pornography, women are exploited and disengaged from their humanity.

According to Kappeler, pornographic representation is a distinctly male way of viewing the world that inevitably reduces the subjectivity of others to the status of mere cultural object. The real subject of pornography is the male viewer or "spectator in front of the picture" who vicariously "possesses" the women, often by identifying with the male (the "bearer of the phallus") in the photograph or film (Berger 1977, p. 54; Giles 1977, p. 55–57). Linda Williams (1989a) adds that "the very fact that a discursive relationship is established to an *image*, rather than a flesh-

and-blood body . . . is what seems most significant" (p. 92); pornography represents "a lack of ability to imagine a relation to the other in anything but the phallic terms of self" (p. 114).[7] Thus, Kappeler believes that pornographic representational practices are inherently opposed to genuine communication.

LIBERTARIAN FEMINISM

Although not a comprehensive philosophical and political perspective, libertarian feminism developed at least partially in response to perceived limitations of the radical feminist position on sexuality and pornography. Like radical feminism, libertarian feminism takes "women's standpoint" as the basis for developing reliable knowledge. However, libertarian feminists believe that radical feminists have overemphasized the experience of women's victimization. They argue that women's experience of pornography and sexuality "is not as universally victimizing" as radical feminists believe since most women would define a large proportion of their sexual experiences as consensual (Duggan et al. 1985, p. 145; Snitow 1983; Vance 1984). They point out that even many women who work in the sex industry do not define themselves as victims (Delacoste & Alexander 1988). Libertarian feminists find it ironic that radical feminism, which claims to take "women's standpoint," seems so foreign to many women.

In contrast to radical feminists, who emphasize the problem of violence against women, libertarian feminists emphasize the sexual repression of women and sexual minorities (for example, lesbians and gays, sadomasochists, transsexuals). The objective of libertarian feminists is to advance women's sexual liberation, and according to their vision of liberation, the essential feature of sexuality should not be emotional intimacy per se, but the exchange of physical, especially genital, pleasure (Ferguson 1984). Sexual freedom involves transgressing "socially respectable categories of sexuality and refusing to draw the line on . . . politically correct sexuality" (p. 109). The ideal sexual relationship should take place between equal and consenting partners who "negotiate to maximize one another's sexual pleasure and satisfaction by any means they choose" (p. 109; Cohen 1986). According to libertarian feminists, women who only experience sexual feelings in a romantic or committed relationship are expressing "a hidden form of alienation rather than a superior ability to integrate sex and love" (Willis 1982a, p. 13; Ellis et al. 1986). While conservatives and radical feminists may not agree on what the appropriate sexual norms should be, libertarian feminists are concerned that the "unfortunate result" of their antipornography stance "is a strengthening of the idea of sexual norms" (Williams 1989a, p. 20). "Are feminists to declare themselves against representations of fellatio, against being on their knees during sex, against anything other than absolutely egalitarian forms of mutual love and affection? Indeed, what forms of sex *are* egalitarian?" (p. 25).

Libertarian feminists also believe that radical feminists have conflated sex and violence, violent pornography and pornography, and pornography and sex, and have thus oversimplified "complex relationships that involve both similarity and difference" (Vance & Snitow 1984, p. 128). For example, in its extreme form some radical feminists suggest that every act of heterosexual intercourse is rape "even if it feels nice because every man has power and privilege over women, whether he uses it blatantly or subtly" (Deevy 1975, p. 24). Similarly, Dworkin (1987) maintains that intercourse becomes a means by which men dominate women "inside" their bodies; in intercourse women are inevitably exploited and vulnerable because the act inherently involves entry, penetration, and occupation. She also describes women's experience with pornography as analogous to Jews' experience of Nazism (1981). And Kappeler (1986) asserts that "with lovers like men, who needs torturers?" (p. 214).

Thus libertarian feminists believe that what began as a radical feminist critique of "hard-core," violent pornography (and the claim that this form was exceedingly common) was expanded to mean that all pornographic representation was both metaphorically and literally violent (Duggan et al. 1985; Vance & Snitow

1984). Women's victimization and sexual suffering became equated with women's sexuality itself, and pornography and pornographic fantasy were seen as lacking any positive "meaning or resonance for women" (Snitow 1985, p. 117). Libertarian feminists acknowledge that the power-laden terrain of sexual interaction poses risks and dangers, but they believe that women can be autonomous agents of their own sexuality and that they are capable of negotiating this terrain for their own purposes (Snitow 1983; Vance 1984).

In addition, libertarian feminists find the radical feminist explanation of how pornography socializes or conditions male sexual fantasy and behavior to be overly simplistic and mechanistic (Ellis et al. 1986; English 1980). They believe that this approach, which adopts the learning theory of behavioristic psychology, reduces male motivation to an unreflective or automatic attitudinal or behavioral response that results from exposure to pornography, and ignores the way in which the symbolic categories implicit in pornography are mediated by individual subjectivity. In contrast, libertarian feminists prefer psychoanalytic explanations of male motivation, although they adopt a feminist-oriented version sensitive to gender-power issues (see Chodorow 1990). They argue that pornography may bring to the surface sexual feelings and fantasies that have been driven underground by a sexually repressive culture, and that men's aggressive fantasies may be a response to some repressed or unconscious threat, fear or anxiety about women, or feeling of sexual inadequacy (English 1980; Williams 1989a; Willis 1982a). For instance, Nancy Waring (1986) suggests that "Hollywood films are shaped by male fear of female sexuality. . . . Men dominate the representational system to reduce their feelings of dread. Women's bodies are objectified, their voices silenced, and their desire is thus subjected to men's" (pp. 96–97). In addition, libertarian feminists sympathize with the view that pornography may have a cathartic effect—that is, it may reduce viewers' sexually aggressive impulses (McCormack 1985b).

Although they do advance some criticisms of male-produced

pornography, libertarian feminists' overriding desire to transcend sexual repression leads them to view pornography as a progressive cultural force (Ehrenreich et al. 1986; Rubin et al. 1981; Willis 1982b). According to Duggan et al. (1985), pornography conveys messages other than the hatred of women. It "flout[s] conventional sexual mores, . . . ridicule[s] sexual hypocrisy and . . . under-score[s] the importance of sexual needs. . . . It advocates sexual adventure, sex outside of marriage, sex for no other reason than pleasure, casual sex, anonymous sex, group sex, voyeuristic sex, illegal sex, [and] public sex" (p. 145). These ideas are appealing to some women who may interpret them as legitimizing their feelings of "sexual urgency or desire to be sexually aggressive."

Libertarian feminists find the analysis of feminist film theorists valuable and believe pornographic representation can be a vehicle for women's sexual liberation (Duggan 1989; Gordon 1984; Waring 1986). They see it as providing an opportunity to investigate how sexuality is constructed, and believe it would be a mistake to leave this realm exclusively to men. Libertarian feminists argue for the "possibility and desirability of women's active agency in relation to patriarchal cultural symbols" and encourage "the use of pornographic images for learning more about the workings of desire" (Waring 1986, pp. 91, 103; Webster 1981). Such a pursuit, however, entails women's complicity in their own objectification since they "have learned to associate their sexuality with domination by the male gaze," and this position inevitably involves "a degree of masochism in finding their objectification erotic" (Kaplan 1983a, p. 324). By an analysis of pornographic images on a frame-by-frame basis, libertarian feminists believe women viewers can effectuate a "more active interaction with the material" and acquire "a 'reading against the grain' that will give [them] information about [their] positioning as spectators" (Gordon 1984, p. 194; Kaplan 1983b, p. 32). Libertarian feminists see radical feminists as fostering a climate of censorship and repression of pornographic representation that will inhibit women's discovery of sexual pleasure in film. "When inquiry into the male fantasies that dominate the representational system is discouraged, so is inquiry into classes of fantasy that are less likely to achieve representation—fantasies of sexual minorities and all women" (Waring 1986, pp. 106–7). "The [radical] feminist rhetoric of abhorrence has impeded discussion of almost everything but the question of whether pornography deserves to exist at all" (Williams 1989a, pp. 4–5).

Williams (1989a) analyzes the development of the "hard-core" film genre from early primitive stag films to the more contemporary feature-length narrative (that is, plot-oriented) films and videos.[8] She views "hard-core" pornography as a film genre that attempts to reveal the "truth" of sex itself through the "involuntary confession" of bodies in spasms of "real" pleasure—in a "frenzy of the visible" (p. 50). But Williams notes that "hard-core pornography is *not* self-evident truth; it is a system of representations with its own developmental history and its own historically changing gender relations. The most central feature of this history has been the increasing problematization of that seemingly natural and universal thing called sex" (p. 267).

According to Williams, early stag films avoided dealing with female sexual pleasure. Male viewers could derive pleasure from investigating women's bodies without having to be concerned about women's pleasure. Later feature-length films such as *Deep Throat* (1972) and *The Opening of Misty Beethoven* (1975), which emerged in the context of the so-called "sexual revolution" and the "scientific" revelations about women's orgasmic capacity and sexual preferences, made sexual satisfaction problematic. In these films, sexual satisfaction was presented "as a problem that a greater knowledge of sexuality [would] 'solve' " (Williams 1989a, p. 152). However, the solutions were generally constructed from the dominant male point of view—a utopia of "different varieties, quantities, and qualities of sexual pleasure," or to use the vernacular, "diff'rent strokes for diff'rent folks" (p. 152).

Until recently, romance novels had been one of the few sources of sexually oriented material for women. Because women's sexuality has traditionally been connected with love and affection, and male sexuality has often not accommodated itself to women's emotional and sexual desires, "unsatisfied female sexuality . . . [has sought] its satisfaction in the fantasy world" of the Harlequin romance formula (Soble 1986, p. 95). Here, "the usual relationship is reversed: woman is subject, man, object. . . . He is the knowable other, a sexual icon whose magic is maleness" and whose primitive sexuality can be tamed by "true love" (Snitow 1983, p. 248; see Farrell 1986; Hazen 1983). Traditionally, these novels portrayed the heroines as "good girls" who were not really aware of their sexual desires and who thus retained their female virtue while negotiating sexual situations. More recently, however, the romance novel formula has begun to change. The new heroine is more self-consciously sexual, actively seeking to satisfy her sexual desire and taste for adventure (Williams 1989a). Carol Thurston (1987) contends that this change has occurred in response to female readers' dissatisfaction with the more passive image of the traditional heroine.

Like the new romance novels, 1980s pornographic films and rental home videos have introduced a new female perspective or "female gaze" (Leo 1987; Squire 1985; Williams 1989a). Some of these films/home videos were produced by Candida Royalle, a former female pornography star who formed "Femme Productions," a company which has attempted to develop pornography that appeals to women. These films/home videos are less focused on genitals and are more plot-oriented, providing an emotional context and motivation for sex. They include older women, and portrayals of mothers, and of more married couples in sex scenes, as well as more kissing, foreplay, afterplay, and attention to women's sexual pleasure. The home videos in particular are often oriented to couples for use as marital aids and as stimuli to lovemaking. Thus, as Williams notes, "it is no longer for men alone to decide what is, or is not, exciting in pornography. . . . Women's desires are now addressed as different from men's, but not so different as to belong outside the economy of desire altogether" (pp. 73, 264). These films portray female protagonists as experimenting with a variety of sexualities, including lesbianism and sadomasochism.

Unlike radical feminists, libertarian feminists posit a separation between fantasy and behavior, and they thus view pornography as a safe place to investigate female sexuality. For instance, Kate Ellis (1985) asserts that "fantasy lives in a domain of its own" and "corresponds *in no way whatsoever* with what I actually enjoy in sex itself" (p. 13). And Lisa Duggan and Ann Snitow (1984) suggest that "in fantasy, we are in control . . . we can flirt with the forbidden, the humiliating and the dangerous . . . [and] test the boundaries of our feelings in ways that might terrify us in real life" (p. 65). In direct opposition to Kappeler's (1986) radical feminist position, libertarian feminists argue that "what we need even more than women against pornography are women pornographers— or eroticists—[who will enable] feminist sexuality [to] confront misogyny with new images" (English 1980, p. 50).

The apparent interest among women in the new "women's pornography" (including films/videos, *Playgirl*, male dancers) reinforces libertarian feminists' claims that radical feminists do not speak for all women. However, libertarian feminist analysis is not without its own conceptual problems. Ilene Philipson (1984) observes that many women would reject libertarian feminists' normative position that characterizes women who desire to integrate love and sex as alienated. Libertarian feminists assume that "human sexuality is a need that is best filled by a maximum of sexual pleasure" rather than "a depth of caring, sensual satisfaction, mutual personal development, and human connection" (Cohen 1986, pp. 76, 85). Rosemarie Tong (1974) adds that "the fact that so many lesbians who practice S & M scoff at the . . . affectional sex they used to enjoy" suggests that their sexual relationships have become more restrictive rather than more liberating (p. 178). Furthermore, Ilene Philipson (1984) notes that the libertarian feminist tendency to dichotomize sexual relations as either repressed or liberated is overly simplistic, as is their implicit reliance on a "drive theory" of sexuality, whereby sexuality is either discharged or repressed. She also suggests that the libertarian concern about antipornography activists turning feminism into a form of "moralistic prudery in which the fear of sexual violence dominates and subsumes the quest for sexual pleasure," and the libertarian view that the enjoyment of pornography represents resistance to a society that "would allow no sexual pleasure at all" (Willis 1982b, pp. 16–17; Rubin et al. 1981), seem overdrawn given contemporary sexual norms. Joan Hoff (1989) characterizes this view as "stemming from the *fear of not being liberal in a conservative era*" (p. 34).

The libertarian feminist approach to the issue of "consent" has also been criticized. For example, the insistence that all consensual sex is acceptable ignores the fact that "consent" may involve "hidden power structures that place women in unequal (hence coercive) positions" (Ferguson 1984, p. 110). Even lesbian relationships sometimes involve nonegalitarian modes of interaction and emotional and physical abuse (Lobel 1986). Furthermore, while libertarian feminists claim to reject an "anything goes" or "do your own thing" approach to sexuality (Vance & Snitow 1984, p. 133), they seem to romanticize as rebellious and progressive all sexual portrayals that seem culturally deviant or that are on the sexual fringe of society (Cohen 1986). For instance, Snitow's (1983) assertion that pornographic themes involving "servants fucking mistresses, old men fucking young girls, [and] guardians fucking wards" are valuable because traditional sexual restrictions "all are deliciously sacrificed, dissolved by sex" is unconvincing, if not ludicrous or pernicious (p. 256; see Waring 1986). Similarly, the characterization of *Deep Throat* as a positive cultural product merely because it portrays a woman actively seeking sexual pleasure through oral sex with multiple partners (Duggan et al. 1985; Ehrenreich et al. 1986) is insensitive to the coercion that was involved in the film's production (Lovelace & McGrady 1980; see Chapter 2).

CONCLUSION

The feminist pornography debate has tended to polarize around the radical and libertarian positions. Although both radical and libertarian feminists agree that patriarchal institutions and values are oppressive and that traditional "male-defined sexuality is inappropriate to women," they disagree over what constitutes appropriate "personal and political relations and sexual liberation" (Cohen 1986, p. 76).

Radical feminists emphasize the victimization of women and advocate a political program that attacks the sources of institutionalized violence against women. Although they believe the state is dominated by patriarchal interests and values, their overriding concern with the harm of pornography leads them to support legal measures to protect women (see Chapter 7). But as we have pointed out, radical feminists who support legal remedies find common ground with traditional conservative opponents of pornography who do not share feminists' general world-view or broader social and political agenda.

Libertarian feminists, on the other hand, believe that radical feminist strategies against pornography will continue to be co-opted by conservatives, as they appeared to be during the Meese Commission hearings. Libertarian feminists are stridently anticensorship, and they are optimistic that feminists' creative involvement with pornography will advance women's sexual liberation. However, libertarian feminism may leave women vulnerable to the continued dominance of patriarchy in the sphere of sexuality. Libertarian feminists find common ground with traditional civil libertarians, including representatives of the pornography industry, who tend to discount concerns about sexual violence and who appear willing to allow the market of consumer preferences to determine what sexually explicit materials will be available, even if such materials convey misinformation about female sexuality and demean, objectify, and threaten women.

NOTES

1. This chapter is based on ideas originally developed in Ronald Berger, Patricia Searles, and Charles Cottle (1990a, 1990b).

2. Categorizing theories is always difficult because of the overlap that sometimes exists between them, and because theory itself is

continuously changing (Jagger 1983). In addition, the formal theoretical arguments articulated by individuals may not necessarily coincide with their own self-identified affiliation, and there may be elements of an author's work that fall into different theoretical domains.

3. Males who believe in rape myths and who hold traditional gender role orientations are more likely to engage in sexual aggression (Koss et al. 1985; Wilson et al. 1983). In addition, a majority of both male and female high school and college students (though males more than females) consider force in sexual relations acceptable under certain conditions—for example, if a woman gets a man "sexually excited" (Goodchilds & Zellman 1984), and about 35 percent of college males admit they might rape if they thought they could get away with it (Malamuth 1981a).

4. According to Herman (1988), "the best currently available data indicate that for women, the risk of being raped is approximately one in four, and that for girls, the risk of sexual abuse by an adult is approximately one in three" (p. 695; see Russell 1984). In addition, about 25 percent of college males reported using some form of coercion to achieve sexual relations with women (Koss et al. 1987; see Berger et al. 1986).

5. See Franklin Mark Osanka and Sara Lee Johann (1989) for examples. In a survey conducted by Russell (1982), 10 percent of the women reported being upset by husbands, lovers, etc., trying to get them to perform acts they read about or saw in pornography. See Alan Soble (1986) for a critique of Diana Russell's findings.

6. For discussions of the domestic and international sex trafficking of women and children, see Barry (1979, 1988) and Ann Wolbert Burgess and Marieanne Lindequist (1984).

7. Williams's observations are made in reference to the stag film genre of pornography. Kappeler would attribute such characteristics to all pornography.

8. Williams defines "hard-core" pornography as "the visual (and sometimes aural) representation of living, moving bodies engaged in explicit, usually unfaked, sexual acts with a primary intent of arousing viewers" (p. 30).

4

Other Feminist Perspectives on Pornography: Liberal, Marxist, Socialist, and Black Feminism

Because they were expressly concerned with issues of sexuality, radical feminism and libertarian feminism emerged as the focal theoretical perspectives within which the feminist antipornography and anticensorship positions were articulated. These two perspectives, however, do not exhaust the feminist theoretical frameworks that can be brought to bear on the issue of pornography. In this chapter, we broaden the controversy by evaluating the implications of feminist theories that have not yet been as central to the pornography debate: liberal, Marxist, socialist and black feminism.[1]

LIBERAL FEMINISM

Liberal feminism makes the same epistemological and ontological assumptions as the more general liberal tradition. In contrast to radical feminism, liberal epistemology posits a dualism between facts and values and presumes it is possible for one to observe the social world without the subjective biases generally associated with questions of value. Liberalism is decidedly positivist in its reliance on "objective" rules of verification and falsification that require "independence from the 'subjective' values, interests and emotions" of the observer (Jaggar 1983, p. 356). This objectivity is available to both men and women and is not seen as inherently "masculine." Thus, no special status is reserved for the standpoint of women.

In contrast to radical feminism, liberal ontology understands individuals as atomistic entities, separate from and superior to society (Jaggar 1983; Wolin 1960). Indeed, society is merely the aggregate of the individuals who compose it, and it is neither groups nor society but individuals who are the repositories of "rights," the bearers of obligations, and the victims of harm. Historically, the liberal tradition has advanced the cause of individual rights in an effort to establish a private sphere in which individual liberties are secure from state and societal interference. Unfettered by these restrictions, the inherent rationality of individuals allows them to achieve personal fulfillment through the pursuit of their interests in a competitive marketplace. In its eighteenth- and nineteenth-century formulations, liberal theory advanced laissez-faire economics as the best means of advancing the interests of the individual. Twentieth-century liberalism, however, has increasingly endorsed governmental regulation of economic life as the preferred way to accomplish this goal.

Thus contemporary liberalism has provided "a philosophical rationale for a gradual enlargement" of government responsibilities to help individuals exercise their rights and pursue their self-interests (Jaggar 1983, p. 34). It asserts that it is "the right of all individuals . . . to be given the opportunity to attain a position in society commensurate with their capabilities" without being discriminated against on the basis of group membership (Macridis 1983, p. 25). Liberal *feminists* have demanded that "liberal ideals" be applied to women as well as men, and that "laws . . . not grant . . . women fewer rights than . . . men" (Jaggar 1983, p. 35). Liberal feminists are primarily concerned that sex discrimination places restrictions "on women *as a group*, without regard to their individual wishes, interests, abilities or merits" (p. 176). Whereas "a man is judged on his merits as an individual," a woman is "assumed to be limited in certain ways because of her sex. Liberal feminists believe that formal freedoms and liberties have little value if individuals are unable to exercise their rights, develop their natural talents, and pursue their self-interests due to discriminatory social practices. They advocate the entrance of women into the mainstream of society so that women may compete equally with men to obtain their share of scarce societal resources.

For liberals as well as liberal feminists, restrictions upon individual freedom are generally governed by John Stuart Mill's "harm principle": "*the only purpose for which power can be rightfully exercised over any member of a civilized community, against his will, is to prevent harm to others*" (1961, p. 197, emphasis ours). Since liberal theory also posits a dualism between the public and private spheres of social life—a distinction which is often assumed to be a natural divide rather than a product of social forces such as the gender-based division of labor (Taub & Schneider 1982)—state intervention is drawn at the line that demarcates the public from the private. Only in the public realm may the state appropriately regulate individual behavior, and here only after a sufficient showing of harm. The "state is supposed to refrain from intervention in the 'private' lives of individuals and from imposing moral values that threaten individual autonomy" (Jaggar 1983, p. 35).

Thus liberals and liberal feminists view sexuality as a private experience that is clearly separate from what is seen as an appropriate sphere of governmental control. Like libertarian feminists, liberal feminists are concerned about the societal repression or distortion of women's sexuality. They believe that women have had "less sexual liberty than men" and that the "perception of women as sexual objects imposes social penalties on women who do not express their sexuality in a way that is pleasing to men"

(p. 179). This perception "also encourages sexual harassment, makes it difficult for women to be taken seriously in non-sexual contexts, and provides a covert legitimization of rape" (p. 179).

But unlike radical feminists, who view human sexuality as a social construction and not as a biological or "natural" given, liberals assume that humans possess an underlying naturally good sexuality. According to Catharine MacKinnon (1984), Susan Griffin (1981) expresses a liberal feminist view when she conceptualizes *eroticism* as natural and healthy but distorted by the "pornographic mind." Griffin argues that pornography "mistakes," "mis-images," and "mis-represents" this natural sexuality. In contrast, radical feminists see pornography not as a distortion of or "artificial overlay upon an inalterable substratum of essential sexual being," but as sexual reality itself (MacKinnon 1984, p. 326, citing Dworkin 1981). Liberal feminists, therefore, distinguish erotica from pornography. To them, erotica involves images or depictions of "mutually pleasurable, sexual expression" between equal and consenting subjects (Steinem 1980, p. 37); it celebrates the body and contains an aesthetic or affectionate component (Ashley & Ashley 1984). Pornography, on the other hand, treats the body as an object to be controlled or dominated; it portrays sex that is violent, degrading, or dehumanizing.

The pornography debate "presents a special problem for liberal feminists because of their commitment to freedom of expression and the right to privacy" (Jaggar 1983, p. 180). Liberal feminists may not like pornography, "but they have no 'political' grounds" to oppose it without a "direct causal" showing of harm (p. 180). Thus they remain committed to a civil libertarian approach to pornography that prohibits the banning or censoring of pornography. Neither conservative moral arguments, nor radical feminist analyses, nor social science research (see Chapter 6) has convinced liberals that pornography is harmful and/or that the potential harm of pornography overrides the harm caused by restricting its availability (Durham 1986; McCormack 1985a, 1985b). Therefore liberal feminists, like libertarian feminists, who may dislike misogynist imagery in pornography but appreciate erotica, find a convenient, albeit uneasy, alliance with traditional civil libertarians who tolerate pornography to preserve individual freedom.

On the other hand, feminist critics like Lorenne Clark (1983) believe that traditional liberalism has placed too much emphasis on "negative" liberty—that is, the freedom to do what one wants unimpeded by interference from others (see Berlin 1969). "Negative" liberty stands in contrast to "positive" liberty, which requires "not only that other persons refrain from interference, but that the person with the freedom . . . [be empowered] . . . to get what he or she wants" (Clark 1983, p. 46). According to Clark, liberals' conception of harm has contained a male bias since their demand for freedom in the private realm has helped to preserve male privilege to dominate, control, exploit, and abuse women and children in the family. She argues that the private realm "is the area most in need of loss of privacy . . . [to promote] . . . greater positive liberty and . . . equality for women" and that women's equality cannot be achieved without a diminution of male privilege (p. 50). Thus Clark believes that liberals need to reconceptualize harm in a way that is consistent with gender (and class) equality, and recognize that "negative liberty" must be compromised "until we have achieved a framework of enforceable rules which guarantees equality within both the public and private spheres" (p. 58; see MacKinnon 1984).

MARXIST FEMINISM

The discourse of Marxist feminism is embedded in the more general Marxist tradition. Like radical feminist epistemology, Marxist epistemology makes no pretense to impartiality. It assumes that all knowledge is political and historically determined. Under capitalism, there are two epistemologies: capitalist and working class (Lukacs 1971). Whereas radical feminism adopts "women's standpoint" as a basis for acquiring knowledge, Marxism adopts the class standpoint of the proletariat or working class.

Only in a classless society, Marxists believe, would it be possible to develop "objective" knowledge.

Like radical feminism, Marxism rejects the liberal atomistic view of the individual, but it gives class (as opposed to gender) ontological priority. The class divisions stemming from the capitalist mode of production constitute the primary contradiction in society from which all other social problems are derivative or secondary. Marxist *feminism* concerns itself with gender issues, or the "woman question," but women are not seen as having a common standpoint. Marxist feminists emphasize the commonalities between women and men of the same class and the differences between people of different classes. Gender issues are understood in terms of the kinds of labor men and women perform, the means by which this labor is organized, and the social relations that form as a result of a particular mode of economic production (Jaggar 1983; Messerschmidt 1986; Rafter & Natalizia 1981). To some extent, Marxist feminists accept the distinction made by liberals between the public and private spheres, but view women's unpaid labor in the private realm (for example, procreation, child-rearing, housework) as functional for capitalism since it provides a cost-effective means of reproducing the labor force. Women's condition is seen to be the result of capitalism, not men's dominance over women, and it cannot be substantially improved until capitalism is superceded by a classless society.

Wilhelm Reich (1972) offered an early Marxist formulation on the "pornography question" that adopted a psychoanalytic orientation, attributing the desire for pornography to the repression of sexuality that is necessitated by capitalism. In his view, sexual repression fosters a passive personality structure that conforms to the discipline and alienation of the workplace. Reich stipulated a distinction between sexual activities engaged in because people are repressed and sexual activities engaged in by those unencumbered by restrictive social norms. He believed that the desire for pornography (as well as rape, homosexuality, and sexual promiscuity) arose when people were prevented from "attaining natural, spontaneous, and satisfying sexual relations"

(Soble 1986, p. 11). Thus Reich, like liberals, assumed the existence of a "naturally" good sexuality, and like libertarian feminists, a sexuality that was either repressed or liberated.

More recent Marxist-oriented analyses view sexuality and pornography not in terms of a "repression model," but as commodities that are socially constructed through the capitalist mode of production (Ashley & Ashley 1984; Foucault 1980; Soble 1986; Steele 1985). In capitalist society, material objects or commodities are produced to be exchanged in the marketplace, not to be used by the immediate producer.[2] Moreover, the dynamics of capitalist production involve a continual expansion of the commodity form into ever-increasing areas of society. As Williams (1989b) notes, contemporary capitalist society "consumes images even more avidly than it consumes objects," and "it no longer matters what the actual use-value of a commodity is so long as it *appears* useful to the consumer" (p. 206). Through advertising, packaging, and other forms of "aesthetic illusion," objects are made desirable irrespective of their actual function or use-value.[3] Thus the mass commercialization of pornographic imagery— "sex as visual pleasure and spectator sport"—transforms the use-value of women's bodies into objects of exchange, and "the very insubstantiality" of what is purchased feeds back upon individuals' needs and renews consumers' willingness to pay for that which they will never own (1989a, p. 121; 1989b, p. 206; see Haug 1986; Marcuse 1964; Sontag 1973).

In addition, the conventional themes in pornography appear analogous to the consumer ethos of capitalism. For instance, in pornography people consume one another sexually as they would consume any other commodity. According to Todd Gitlin (1990), in a society of disposable products, sex is a commodity that can "be turned in for next year's model" (p. 103). Similarly, the frequent depiction of ejaculating penises (perhaps not coincidentally referred to by pornographers as the "money shot") that present men as "limitlessly endowed with the universal fluid currency which can be spent without loss," and the unlimited orgasmic ("spending") capacity of women in pornography, are viewed by some analysts as metaphors for a consumer society (Marcus 1974, p. 22; Williams 1989b).

Alan Soble (1986) applies a Marxist perspective in an attempt to understand men's attraction to or desire for pornography. He views the workplace regimen of capitalist production as requiring the psychic and physical desensitization of the laborer, whereby bodily sensations that do not contribute to the production process are deemphasized if not essentially eliminated. This desensitization includes a loss of spontaneity, creativity, and playfulness, as well as a loss of the pleasure provided by the nonvisual senses. The desensitized laborer engaged in long hours of nonsensuous activity develops a sexuality that emphasizes a utilitarian release of tension. Women become defined by their sexual function and are objectified as mere outlets of male sexual desire. Women's body parts, often portrayed in pornography as dismembered from the whole, provide the visual stimuli that the desensitized male needs for sexual arousal. Pornography is used as an aid to masturbation that helps workers release their sexual tensions and ease their return to an unsatisfying job (Betzold 1977; see Gitlin 1990; Lippert 1977).[4]

On the consumption side, Soble (1986) argues that the "commodification" of pornography involves two contradictory cultural elements—a conservative sexual morality, which perpetuates restrictive norms, and a liberal morality (in part promoted by the "pop psych" and health industries), which encourages an active sex life for the "healthy" individual (see Kovel 1990). But since pornography is not necessarily tied to the acting out of fantasy with sexual partners, the use of pornography to enhance masturbatory pleasure "satisfies, in a convoluted way, both conservative prohibitions (no 'real' sexual activity is engaged in . . .) and liberal norms ('if it feels good, do it')" (Soble 1986, pp. 76–77).

Contrary to radical feminism, Soble argues that men's enjoyment of pornography is not an expression of males' power, but their lack of power, a defensive adaptation to the social advances of women (see Schipper 1980). Soble's analysis thus resembles the libertarian feminist view that men's consumption of pornography is related to their fear of women. According to Soble, women's decreased willingness to accommodate themselves to male sexuality has contributed to males' sense of sexual powerlessness. Pornography restores men's sense of control over their sexuality by offering them a fantasy world of fully accommodating women who are interested in sex on men's terms without the entanglements, commitments, and obligations of a real-life partner. On the other hand, Soble notes that men's consumption of pornography contradicts prevailing notions of masculinity since masturbation violates masculine performance standards ("real men" have sex with real women).

In fashioning a so-called Marxist defense of pornography, Soble argues that the social context of its production and consumption, rather than its actual depictions, determines its meaning—that is, whether it is degrading, dehumanizing, and so on. While he is willing to concede that much, if not most, contemporary pornography is degrading, he believes that the material conditions for nonsexist pornography would exist in an ideal "communist" society—that is, one without class- and gender-based power differences. He argues that the negative themes in much contemporary pornography are historical-empirical facts, not universal truths that follow from a definition of pornography's inherent nature. In a communist society of "collective and freely associated people" (p. 141), the material conditions would exist for a nonexploitative, nonalienating pornography. From the standpoint of production, people would "choose freely to make pornography" (p. 132). Its production would be "undertaken for its own sake,'" not for mass marketing, and it would be "directed and managed by those involved as labor," with wages collectively determined. "No one's body . . . [would be] commodified by an exchange relationship" (p. 132). On the consumption side, Soble believes that under communism the viewing of pornography would be a perfectly valid means to appreciate "the ability of the [pornography] performer to satisfy the principles of art" (p. 143).

Nevertheless, the policy implications of Soble's thesis are unclear since his defense of pornography assumes the existence of an ideal "communist" society. While libertarian feminists could read his work as supportive of the need for alternative feminist erotica, Soble's perspective would not necessarily preclude strategies taken against contemporary patriarchal pornography. Soble, however, differs from libertarian feminists in that he believes changes in the material conditions of society must precede the transformation of pornography.

Although some Marxists have advocated "progressive censorship" to repress conservative or reactionary ideas (Marcuse 1969), most Marxists have feared that restrictions on pornography under capitalism would increase state power to stifle political expression and dissent (Jaggar 1983). Marxist *feminists* have been critical of special protective legislation for women because they believe that such legislation is a form of legal paternalism that inevitably has discriminatory effects (Rafter & Natalizia 1981). Such legal paternalism has legitimized limitations on hours women have been allowed to work, or has totally excluded women from certain occupations, because of females' presumed physical inferiority or inherent domestic nature (Taub & Schneider 1982).[5] It has also criminalized adolescent females' sexual conduct (while ignoring males') because of a perceived need to protect female virtue (Chesney-Lind 1989). Thus, Marxist feminists would likely dispute radical feminists' call for antipornography legislation designed to protect women. They believe that rape is related to the general level of violence in society, and results more from economic deprivation than from male socialization (Schwendinger & Schwendinger 1983). Eliminating rape, like other "street crimes," requires improving the economic circumstances of the population of potential offenders.

SOCIALIST FEMINISM

Socialist feminism attempts to synthesize the best insights of radical feminism and Marxism while simultaneously avoiding problems associated with each. In contrast to Marxism, which takes class as primary, and in contrast to radical feminism, which takes gender as primary, socialist feminism emphasizes the mutual interdependence between these two sources of inequality and oppression (Jaggar 1983; Messerschmidt 1986).

Unlike Marxism, socialist feminism gives women, because of their distinct social position, a special epistemological standpoint. It holds that an adequate theory of knowledge must represent the standpoint of women. But unlike radical feminism, socialist feminism does not assume that women's standpoint is "available to all [women] and only to women" (Jaggar 1983, p. 387). It rejects radical feminism's "false universalization of women's experience," and argues that although men may "find it more difficult to comprehend [women's] perspective," they are in principle capable of conveying women's standpoint.

According to Jaggar, socialist feminism's contribution to the analysis of women's condition is not the discovery of "new facts," but the promise of "a new theoretical framework" capable of demonstrating "the quality and systematic interrelations of the now-familiar facts" (pp. 316–7). For socialist feminism, capitalism is not a genderless mode of economic production. Patriarchy, the system of male dominance, is a constitutive part of the economic foundation of society, not a mere by-product. Patriarchy institutionalizes a system of normative heterosexuality that entails male control over women's labor, sexuality, and procreative capacities (Messerschmidt 1986). Socialist feminism describes capitalism as the sphere of production and patriarchy as the sphere of reproduction, although this characterization may be somewhat artificial as it implies that women's labor (reproduction) is less fundamental and creative than men's labor (production) (Jaggar 1983). Nevertheless, the sexual division of labor creates gendered behavioral styles and character structures (Messerschmidt 1986).

Whereas Soble's Marxist analysis of sexuality emphasizes the sexual alienation of men, socialist feminism offers a theory of sexual alienation from the standpoint of women (Jaggar 1983). Patriarchal capitalism socially constructs women as sexual objects valued primarily for their sexual capital (see Lerner 1986). Women's economic survival often requires them to present themselves as sexually pleasing to men in the labor and/or marriage marketplaces. Women receive the sexual attention of men whether it is welcome or not, and their sexuality is defined by masculine desires and for men's rather than women's enjoyment. Thus women's sexuality is socially constructed first for exchange in the marketplace and second for ownership by the (male) employer and/or husband.

In this process, women are alienated because they internalize the male-defined "identification of their selves with their bodies," often with only "the fetishized parts of their bodies" (Jaggar 1983, p. 309). Women also separate themselves from their bodies by treating their appearance as "recalcitrant nature" that can be overcome by a myriad of beauty aids. Having internalized the attitude of men, women develop a "feminine narcissism" and take erotic pleasure in defining themselves as sex objects; they revel in their bodies as "beautiful object[s] to be gazed at and decorated" (Bartky 1982, pp. 131–2). Thus, women are sexually alienated not only because they "are not free to express their sexual preferences," but also because they cannot discover what their sexual preferences are (Jaggar 1983, p. 309). Furthermore, women are alienated from each other because competition for male sexual attention prevents them from perceiving their shared interests and exchanging their sexuality among themselves (see Irigaray 1985).

Although an explicitly socialist feminist analysis of pornography has yet to be developed, the socialist feminist critique of sexuality implies a critical stance toward much contemporary pornography. Pornography can be seen as reinforcing patriarchal institutions, including the prevailing form of male domination over female sexuality. For instance, Burstyn (1985a) observes that the "initial insights of the feminist critique of pornography were important . . . [for an] . . . understanding of masculinist institutions [because they showed] how sexist values were being reinforced even under the supposedly liberating guise of the 'sexual revolution' " of the 1960s (p. 157). Socialist-oriented analysts are often critical of the "commodification" of sexuality associated with the capitalist mode of production (Gitlin 1990; Mura 1987). Although many socialists once believed that the sexual liberation movement posed a challenge to the workplace alienation of capitalist life, some lament that its progressive impulses have been co-opted through the mass marketing of sex (Betzold 1977; Kovel 1990). On the other hand, some self-identified socialist feminists have articulated a libertarian feminist view that emphasizes the progressive aspects of pornography and its potential role in subverting patriarchal institutions and values (Ehrenreich et al. 1986; English 1980; Rubin et al. 1981).

Insofar as socialist feminism attempts to integrate insights of other feminist perspectives, it may offer the most promising feminist framework for recharacterizing the feminist pornography debate and perhaps for moving beyond the current impasse. Following Robin West (1989), a socialist feminist approach would begin with the assumption that pornography is a "profoundly contradictory" phenomenon (p. 109; see Ferguson 1984). West (1989) argues that feminists should acknowledge women's varying experiences with pornography: some women have felt victimized or harmed by pornography, others have felt liberated by it, and still others have felt both victimized and liberated. (The reader will recall public opinion data reviewed in Chapter 1 which indicates that a majority believe that pornography has both positive *and* negative effects.) According to West, these experiences are indications of the contradictions in pornographic texts themselves, which in turn reflect the contradictions in patriarchal society where women's experience of sexuality has been neither universally negative nor positive. Men, too, have had contradictory experiences with pornography—a point we will take up in more detail in the next chapter.

Thus the different feminist perspectives on pornography, which have attempted to explain why pornography is either bad or good, mirror the diverse messages contained in pornography: Some messages may have negative value, some messages may have positive value, and some messages may be ambiguous or contradictory (Downs 1989; West 1989).[6] The contradictory nature of pornography lies in the fact that it contains both a threat and a promise, both potential risks and dangers as well as potential benefits and opportunities. The threat (as suggested by radical feminists) is the violence, subordination, and limitations on women's sexuality that are represented in pornography. The promise (as suggested by libertarian feminists) is the potential for sexual liberation and the opportunity to insist that "pornography actually deliver on its utopian promises: that 'sexually explicit texts' depict what is truly pleasurable, and what is truly beneficial to women" (West 1989, p. 126).

Both radical and Marxist feminist perspectives tend to view the commercialization of mass culture, including pornography, in *instrumental* terms. That is, dominant groups (for example, male capitalists) are seen as using cultural forms of communication to dominate, control, and instill false consciousness among subordinate groups (for example, women and workers). But although pornography is dominated by patriarchal capitalist values and institutions, some argue that "important degrees of freedom remain for the production of meanings that are independent of either the logic of exchange value or the dominant cultural sensibility" (Gottdiener 1985, p. 998). Ideological control of subordinate groups is never complete, and there is constant struggle over the meanings of cultural objects. Any commodity, including pornography, can be "transfunctionalized"—that is, the symbolic meanings associated with its use can be modified (Krampen 1979). Subordinate groups can take an active role in relation to cultural symbols and work "outside the mainstream . . . [to] create meanings for their own expressive purposes" (Gottdiener 1985, p. 996). Among the multiple messages in pornography are the "legitimating promises that, if read expansively, can be turned against the privilege that produced them, carrying us closer to the utopian world beyond the privilege" (West 1989, p. 126). Hence libertarian feminists argue for creating alternative meanings through feminist erotica.

However, capitalist producers of mass culture (for example, pornographers) respond to alternative meanings (for example, feminist erotica) by marketing them in ways that trivialize or negate their transformative potential or radical message (Gottdiener 1985). As radical feminists have suggested, women pornographers may make little difference, for by demanding that pornography deliver on its promise of actual benefit and real sexual pleasure, feminists run the risk of reinforcing rather than dismantling the oppressive qualities of patriarchal culture (West 1989). The attempt to develop a "softer" pornography, or feminist erotica, may merely provide pornographers with new ideas for expanding the profitable markets for the commercialization of sexuality, as well as encourage individuals to "discover" their sexuality through superficial interaction with mass-produced cultural symbols rather than through egalitarian communicative relationships with other human beings. As long as pornography is consumed like any other product, the diversification of images may deny individuals "the freedom to choose what would ultimately nourish [them]"—the freedom from false desires and from the illusion that consumption is equivalent to freedom itself (Mura 1987, p. 18; Sontag 1973). According to Joel Kovel (1990), "a nation of pornography consumers is no different, politically speaking, than a nation of heroin junkies," for pornography diminishes peoples' "capacity for critical resistance" (p. 164).

Thus, a socialist feminist perspective must be cognizant of the contradictory potential of feminist erotica, both how it may influence and how it may be co-opted by mainstream pornography. At this point in time, it would be more constructive to focus not on the normative debate (whether pornography and/or feminist erotica is bad or good), but on an analysis of the contradictions inherent in the production, distribution, and consumption of sexually explicit materials.

Although socialist feminists, like Marxists, are generally cautious of special protective legislation for women, many would support nonlegal strategies vis-à-vis pornography such as educational and consciousness-raising efforts and civil disobedience against the purveyors of misogynist pornographic imagery (see Chapter 8). More importantly, socialist feminists emphasize strategies not directly related to pornography but designed to improve the condition of women in other areas of society. For instance, Varda Burstyn (1985b) advocates "positive strategies" for women including economic and social programs for women and youth (for example, full employment, equal pay for equal work, affirmative action, child care, battered-women shelters); general sex education; reproductive and erotic rights for women and sexual minorities; democratization of the mass media; and legal protection, improved working conditions, and economic options for sex-industry workers. According to socialist feminists, the problems attributed to pornography are symptomatic of other societal forces that cannot be transformed by a political strategy that focuses on pornography itself.

BLACK FEMINISM

Race-related issues have been a source of division within the feminist community. Women of color have observed that the feminist movement is composed largely of white middle-class women who have neglected the critical importance of race in the oppression of black, Chicana, Asian, and Native American women (Chow 1987; Collins 1986; Garcia 1989; Gardner 1980). As opposed to gender problems as such, women of color have emphasized issues of poverty, education, health care, welfare and immigration reform, and bilingual education. As feminists whose experiences differ from those of white women, feminist women of color make claims to a special epistemological standpoint (Collins 1986). While emphasizing the centrality of race, these feminists analyze the "interlocking nature" of the multiple sources of oppression—race, class, and gender (p. 521; Hooks 1981). Tracey Gardner (1980) encourages white women to "understand that while sexism might be the ultimate oppression for . . . them, it is only *one* of the ways in which women of color are oppressed" (p. 114).

Although black women have not been highly visible in the pornography debate, they appear to have given more attention to the issue than have other women of color. However, many black women have discounted feminists' concerns about pornography, believing that it pales in comparison to other problems and describing antipornography feminism as "an instance of misplaced outrage, a spewing of venom that only white middle-class women can afford" (Tong 1984, p. 156). Others, like libertarian feminists, have viewed pornography as a progressive force, and they have simply desired "equal time" with white women (see Walker 1980). Since many view black solidarity as more important that female solidarity, black women have been concerned that involvement in feminist activity would alienate black men and fragment the black community (Eichelberger 1979).

Black feminists' views on the issue of rape have also differed from those of white feminists. Some have criticized white feminists in the antiviolence movement for emphasizing black males' overrepresentation in crime statistics on rape (Davis 1981), and some have been reluctant to press for greater rape law enforcement because of the history of discrimination against black men (Tong 1984). Furthermore, black (as well as Mexican American) women are less likely than white women to accept "feminist" definitions of rape (Williams & Holmes 1981), even though official crime rates and victimization surveys indicate that black women are more likely than white women to have experienced rape and attempted rape (Searles & Berger 1987). In general, black women have a more narrow definition of rape than white women. They are less likely to define rape as sex without the women's consent, and more likely to qualify their definition of rape according to the female's activities or reputation, the offender's use of force, the victim-offender relationship, and so on (Williams & Holmes 1981). Black women are also more likely to avoid rape when assaulted. They are more likely to have acquired "street smarts," to have been advised by their families to fight back, and to resist when attacked (Bart & O'Brien 1985).

But some black feminists find value in the feminist antipornography movement. For example, Gardner (1980) argues that while pornography is produced and consumed primarily by white men, and while it speaks mainly to their relationships with white women, it is nevertheless relevant to blacks who "have been forced to live under the values of white people" (p. 112). Pornography that utilizes white models reinforces the notion that it is white women who are beautiful. According to Alice Walker (1980), this pornography also provides black men with symbolic access to white women who have been historically "off-limits" to them, thereby allowing them a common bond with white men at women's expense. She notes that this gender solidarity with white men is especially troubling when the pornography black men enjoy demeans black women. Gardner (1980) adds that while white men have attempted to destroy black men's sense of power, black men have attempted to restore their power by exerting domination over black women.

Black feminists find the radical feminist notion of female sexual slavery (see Barry 1979) especially relevant to black women. Given the history of legalized slavery in the United States, the concept of sexual slavery has a more specific status in black feminists' ontology of pornography. Under legalized slavery, black women were treated as chattel for their masters, who raped them with legal impunity and mated them to male slaves to produce the best "stock" (Gardner 1980; Teish 1980). Gardner (1980) adds that white men's treatment of white women can be understood in terms of white men's treatment of black men. She notes that the "inhuman treatment of Black men by white men . . . has a direct correlation to white men's increasingly obscene and inhuman treatment of women . . . in pornography and in real life. . . . White women, working toward their own strength and identity, their own sexuality and independence, have in a sense become 'uppity niggers' " (p. 111).

Pornographic images of black women have reflected notions inherited from slavery. Black women have been viewed as sluts "who could take anything sexually" (p. 111), as animals desiring to be tamed by their masters, or as "Bubbling Brown Sugars who will share their sweetness indiscriminately" (Tong 1984, p. 158). Some black feminists find it particularly disturbing that black men seem to miss the historical connections when they enjoy images of black women in bondage (Gardner 1980; Walker 1980). Such negative stereotypes of black women have been partly responsible for criminal justice officials' tendency to discount black women's accusations of rape and to treat offenders who assault black women more leniently (see LaFree 1989). Black men are also portrayed in pornography in stereotypical ways that derive from the slavery era, when black men were viewed as sexual savages. In pornography the black man "is defined solely by the size, readiness, and unselectivity of his cock, . . . as being capable of fucking anything" (Walker 1980, p. 103). Thus, some black feminists call for all blacks to address the negative imagery in black pornography and other cultural media (Teish 1980).

CONCLUSION

In an attempt to broaden the feminist pornography debate beyond the radical-libertarian feminist controversy, we have considered the implications of liberal, Marxist, socialist, and black feminist perspectives. Notwithstanding the volume of literature on pornography produced by other feminists, liberal feminists constitute the dominant political group within feminism. Liberal feminists believe it is important to distinguish between pornography and erotica, and hope that consumer preferences will change and that erotica will displace pornography in the marketplace. However, they consider sexuality to be a private matter and are cautious about legal regulation in this area.

Compared to liberal feminism, Marxist and socialist feminism remain marginal to the political process in the United States. Both offer critical views of the "commodification" of sexuality and the sexual alienation of men and women in capitalist society. But while they acknowledge the sexism of much contemporary pornography, both share liberal feminism's reluctance to legislate against pornography, and both view pornography as secondary and symptomatic of broader societal forces that must be changed if pornography is to be transformed or eliminated.

Socialist feminism seems to offer the best possibility to re-characterize the feminist pornography debate and move beyond the current impasse. Because it draws on the insights of other perspectives, it is a theoretical framework capable of integrating the best of feminist thought about pornography and analyzing the contradictions inherent in the commercialization of sexually explicit materials.

Finally, the writings of black feminists suggest the importance of analyses of pornography that are sensitive to the interlocking nature of race, class, and gender. Future analyses should avoid the false universalization of women's experience and create a climate that encourages all women (and men) to speak about their understanding of and experience with pornography. It is important that competing theories not become competing ideologies that prevent open dialogue and that constrain feminists from searching outside feminist theory for other theoretical discourses that might provide insight into the social psychological and structural-institutional dimensions of pornography.[7]

NOTES

1. The sections on liberal, Marxist, and socialist feminism in this chapter are based on ideas originally developed in Ronald Berger, Patricia Searles, and Charles Cottle (1990a.)

2. Money becomes the universal equivalent or the embodiment of value through which commodities are exchanged, and objects, which are products of human labor that represent relations between people, take on the appearance of relations between things (Marx 1967).

3. Material commodities also signify to others certain qualities about the consumer. For instance, automobiles are often purchased not only for transportation but to signify to others the owner's social status (Gottdiener 1985).

4. Jim Stodder (1979) notes that employers actually distributed pornographic magazines and films to offshore workers for precisely this reason.

5. Women's current exclusion from armed combat duty is viewed by some as denying women "a crucial test of citizenship" (Taub & Schneider 1982, p. 119).

6. See Gloria Steinem (1986) vs. Barbara Ehrenreich, Elizabeth Hess, and Gloria Jacobs (1986) and Linda Williams (1989a, 1989b) for contradictory interpretations of the thematic message of *Deep Throat*.

7. For instance, in our account of socialist feminism and pornography, we drew upon nonfeminist theories of mass culture (see Gottdiener 1985). Other nonfeminist traditions that should be explored more thoroughly include, among others, semiotics, symbolic anthropology, critical theory, and ethnomethodology. Applications of existentialist feminism and postmodern feminism might also be useful (see Tong 1989).

5

Men's Perspectives
On Pornography

Recently, male writers have begun to respond to the feminist debate by confronting their feelings about and experiences with pornography and by developing their own analyses of it. Michael Kimmel (1990) suggests a number of reasons for men's relative silence on this issue: embarrassment or guilt for having enjoyed pornography, anger at female interference in male privilege, lack of interest in what they perceive to be a non-issue, fear that speaking out will lead to questions about one's masculinity, reluctance to talk openly with one another about their sexual feelings, and confusion about the meaning of masculinity—"what it means to be a 'real man' " in contemporary society (Kimmel 1987a, p. 121).

Men's confrontation with pornography can be situated in the context of an emerging men's movement that has developed largely in response to the contemporary women's movement. The men's movement, like the women's movement, consists of several branches with differing priorities.[1] First, there are those men who are sympathetic to feminism. These men include academic men who are creating feminist-oriented "men's studies" in university and college settings (Brod 1987; Kimmel 1987b; Kimmel & Messner 1989). They are attempting to fill the gap in gender studies by developing analyses of the *male* gender role that have often been absent from women's studies curricula. Pro-feminist men (nonacademic as well as academic) are also involved in political groups, such as the National Organization for Men Against Sexism, that are attempting to develop alternatives to the traditional male role. They believe this role limits men's ability to realize their full human potential. They hope to help men liberate themselves from the confines of masculinity and to "mold men into more benign beings" (Gross 1990, p. 11). Political groups of pro-feminist men also include those with more specific foci, such as Men Against Rape and Men Against Pornography, which are working to eliminate sexual violence.

In contrast, there are men who are reacting against, rather than in support, of feminism (see Kimmel 1987c). Some of these men have a traditional religious-conservative ideology that supports a "return to patriarchy," with its relegation of women to the family for performance of biologically based roles as wives and mothers. Nonreligious organizations such as the National Coalition for Free Men and the National Organization for Men attempt to reassert traditional masculinist values and heal the wounds incurred from a perceived feminist assault. In one writer's words, these men are "unabashedly male-positive, brazenly insensitive, real men . . . [who] hate male feminists, whom they accuse of gender treason" (Gross 1990, p. 12). They feel "wimpified" and "emasculated," and are trying to change laws they believe discriminate against men (for example, child custody and child support laws) (p. 13). Finally, there are groups such as the Mythopoetic Men who celebrate maleness by getting "in touch with their preindustrial masculinity" and meeting "together in nature . . . in the absence of women and civilization (pp. 11, 14) . . . [to] create islands of untainted masculinity and purified pockets of virility . . . that . . . socialize young men to the hardiness appropriate to their gender" (Kimmel 1987c, p. 262).

To a large extent, men writing about pornography have mirrored preexisting analyses. Like women, men do not possess a uniform view on pornography. Some men have expressed traditional views—religious-conservative or civil libertarian (see Chapter 2). Some have expressed ideas consistent with radical feminism, libertarian feminism, or other feminist perspectives (see Chapters 3 and 4; *Changing Men* 1985; Kimmel 1990). However, males' position in society as men has provided them a special perspective or epistemological standpoint that has resulted in unique insights about the ontology of pornography and its meaning to men.

Some men feel that men's experience with pornography has not been adequately understood by antipornography feminists. While some women have felt silenced by pornography, some men have felt silenced by the pornography debate. Fred Small (1985) writes, "When Andrea Dworkin says that 'any defense of pornography is war' against women, I am discouraged from contemplative and free-ranging discussion" (p. 7). Philip Weiss (1990) complains that men who opposed the Dworkin-MacKinnon antipornography ordinance were viewed either as "scumball" consumers or as First Amendment absolutists who supported the expression of all ideas no matter how offensive (for example, Nazism) (p. 93). He believes that men have been allowed little room to express ambivalent feelings about pornography. Some men acknowledge the problems with pornography that have been identified by radical feminists, yet their experience of sexual arousal by pornography leads them to find some of the same value in pornography that libertarian feminists have found (MacDonald 1990; Steinberg 1990). They believe that pornography contains not only misinformation but also useful information about sex, and the fact that they find pornography exciting leaves them feeling grateful for and protective of pornography, as well as embarrassed, guilty, and fearful of being misunderstood.

WHY MEN CONSUME PORNOGRAPHY

Perhaps the most striking feature of men's perspective on pornography is the incongruity between the reality of men's gender privilege and their subjective experience of powerlessness. In the previous chapter, we reviewed Alan Soble's (1986) Marxist view which describes men's sense of powerlessness and use of pornography to enhance masturbatory fantasy as key elements of men's experience with pornography.[2] Other men also emphasize these themes.

Men writing about pornography usually assert that most male consumers are able to separate the fantasy world of pornography, that "utopian kingdom" of ever-ready women and ever-hard men, from the real world (Lopate 1981, p. 211; Steinberg 1990; Weiss 1990). The appeal of pornography lies in its promise of a sexuality free of taboo and restraint, in its ability to transcend "all of life's hesitations and doubts" (Kovel 1990; Lopate 1981, p. 211). According to David Steinberg (1990), pornographic fantasy addresses "unfulfilled desires," the sexual feelings that are unsatisfied in men's lives (p. 54). He argues that most heterosexual men experience their sexual lives in terms of scarcity. Women are often resistant to men's sexual desires—they are disinterested, reluctant, fearful, even repulsed. Men thus have "little opportunity to be desired . . . and appreciated" for their sexual natures (p. 55). Since "women hold the power of rejection," it is hard for most men to see women as powerless (Small 1985, p. 44).[3] In fact, they are socialized to believe that women have the power to confirm their manhood. If women deny men sex, men's self-esteem and sense of masculinity are undermined, and they feel anger at women. Thus men's consumption of pornography is fueled by a "combination of lust and rage," and is an expression not of men's power over women but of their feeling of powerlessness and their sense of sensual aesthetic inferiority (Kimmel 1990, p. 308; MacDonald 1990).[4] Images of lustful, desiring women help men fantasize sexual interactions that soothe their emotional wounds (Steinberg 1990). Warren Farrell (1986) adds that although men have been socialized to view women as *sex* objects, women have been socialized to view men as *success* objects. In our society, one reward for a man's financial success is the acquisition of beautiful women. For men who cannot achieve this ideal of success and who fear rejection by real women, pornography provides access to the beautiful women they cannot attract in real life.

Timothy Beneke (1990) argues that men's experience of pornography cannot be separated from "men's daily social experience of looking at women" (p. 169). Men's normal perceptual routine involves secretive glances, the "stealing" of images of women's bodies (p. 170). He notes that to be caught staring would be embarrassing and humiliating, yet men find it difficult to avoid looking, especially because erotic images regularly intrude into their perceptual field and arouse them involuntarily. Men feel a deep sense of injustice because women have the right to present—and even try to present—a sexy appearance to men, but men must mask their desire to look. Thus pornography, according to Beneke, represents a revenge against women's ability to arouse men against their will. It "cushion[s] men's humiliation" by giving them the freedom to look at women's bodies, and it poses the women in such a way as to "make men feel proud in looking" (p. 174). Scott MacDonald (1990) adds that pornography allows men to support women's desire to not be ogled by providing men "a form of unintrusive leering" (p. 39).

Thus, some men writing about pornography believe it serves a cathartic function: it helps release the "annoying sexual energy" of unsatisfied sexuality, and it provides "a victimless outlet" for the anger and rage engendered by feelings of powerlessness and inferiority (Lopate 1981, p. 212; Steinberg 1990, p. 57; MacDonald 1990). Moreover, some argue that pornography allows men to "reassert their mastery over women" and reassure themselves that they are "still on top" in spite of feminism and the women's movement (Betzold 1977, pp. 45–46).

In addition, some men believe that pornography has educational value (Kimmel 1990). It helps adolescents feel validated sexually and helps us all accept sexuality as normal (Steinberg 1990). It enables men to view and examine women's bodies and sexual functioning without the embarrassment of being observed, and it helps them overcome their fear of being ignorant about how to interact sexually with women (see Di Lauro & Rabkin 1976). It teaches men about sources of female pleasure and helps redirect "traditional male hatred and fear of vaginas . . . toward vaginal appreciation" (Steinberg 1990, p. 57). In addition, the presence of the female in the pornography also allows heterosexual men to examine men's bodies and sexual functioning without defining themselves as homosexual. Men are able to experience the naturalness of male bodily functions (erections and ejaculations) in a culture that associates beauty primarily with females and that leads men to feel insecure about the attractiveness of their bodies. In pornography, women accept and even adore men "despite their personal unattractiveness . . . and . . . their aggressiveness with their semen" (MacDonald 1990, p. 41). Pornography also helps men reduce the guilt and shame that may be associated with their sexual fantasies, and it is used by couples to enhance their sexual experiences and rekindle their sexual passions (Kimmel 1990; Zilbergeld 1990).

Like libertarian feminists, some men writing about pornography draw on psychoanalytic-oriented analyses of males' fear of women.[5] For instance, Gad Horowitz and Michael Kaufman (1987) argue that men become fascinated with women's bodies because they are unconsciously anxious about castration. They become "fixated on the object of fear, those beings who are without penises" (p. 94). In addition, men have been forced to repress the "feminine" (passive, receptive, soft) aspects of their personalities in order to conform to dominant societal views of masculinity. Pornography is thus appealing because the sight of women's bodies confirms one's sense of maleness, and the sight of women in passive, dominated positions confirms one's sense of masculinity. But according to Horowitz and Kaufman, pornography can also be appealing when women are portrayed as sexually aggressive, for then men are offered a safe opportunity to experience a passivity and receptivity in sexual pleasure that is denied them in real life. On the other hand, images of even passive women are threatening to some men who can enjoy pornography only when images of bondage or brutalization portray the active, explicit domination of women. However, mere looking cannot be fulfilling in the long run, and continued viewing results in increased frustration and greater tensions. Hence some men's taste for pornography becomes increasingly sadistic as a means of obtaining mastery over "the object of desire" (p. 99).

Also employing a psychoanalytic perspective, Beneke (1990) suggests that men fear sex with real women because it signals to their unconscious a loss of self, a desire to regress to the infantile union they experienced with their mothers. Pornography helps men defend against this regression by training them to achieve sexual "arousal and gratification with minimal identification with women" (p. 179). Because the tactile elements of arousal present a "greater threat of identification," the visual elements supercede the tactile for many men (p. 182). Thus, like Catharine MacKinnon (1984), Beneke argues that men can have sex with their image of their partner's body even more than with the partner herself. Beneke believes these psychological conflicts lead many men to find the simultaneous experience of nurturance and sex threatening, and hence they tend to view women as either nurturing "madonnas" or lustful "whores."[6] However, he maintains that feminists' understanding of sexual objectification is overly simplistic since it is possible for men to objectify women while also attending to their subjectivity.[7] As he writes, "Being sexually attracted to a woman, in part, means being excited by her body; what is sexist is the inability to simultaneously feel that excitement and accord women the respect and acknowledgment they deserve" (p. 178). What is sexist about pornography, then, is not the visual representation of nude women, but the encouragement "of men to possess a *distorted* knowledge of women as subjects" (our emphasis).

THE DRAWBACKS OF CONSUMPTION

Phillip Lopate (1981) suggests that it is important to distinguish the occasional consumer of pornography from the regular user. The occasional consumer may be a "bachelor aesthete," like himself, or a "married man on moral holiday" (p. 207). But regular users are rather pathetic figures who are hooked on an "anti-aphrodisiac" for "their painfully aroused libidos" (p. 212). These addicts seek out pornography not only for excitement, but "to be put in touch with their sadness," their lack of connection, and "to contemplate the missed opportunities of a lifetime" (p. 208). As with drug addiction, the initial excitement of pornography quickly wears off, leaving the user exhausted, indifferent, even bitter, helplessly caught in an endless and hopeless search for new sources of gratification, with "nowhere to go but back" to the "sludgelike mediocrity" of porn (Kovel 1990, p. 154; Lopate 1981, p. 213; Schipper 1980). David Mura (1987) adds that the pornography addict uses pornography to numb his "psychic pain," but as with drugs, the pain continually reappears, because pornography cannot satisfy his "spiritual hunger" (p. 3, 17).[8]

Although some men acknowledge that women are exploited by pornography (Betzold 1977; Gitlin 1990), some emphasize men's exploitation, since it is women who get paid for making what men pay to see.[9] Lopate (1981) criticizes male consumers only for lacking the imagination "to produce erotic images on their own" (p. 209). He prefers not to consider pornography actors as sex objects, but as performers who "have been elevated into embodiments of the physical life, like dancers" (p. 210–1). Mura (1987), on the other hand, believes that pornography does involve objectification and the reduction of others to "tools of sexual gratification," and argues that a "person engaged in viewing the world pornographically is abusing himself, as well as women" (p. 17, 6).

Other men have criticized even the nonaddictive consumption of pornography and believe that men should recognize the harm of pornography to men as well as to women (Brod 1990). Steinberg (1990) observes that pornography may alienate men from their sexual selves; it may present images of sexually desirable men that some men feel they cannot live up to.[10] Or, as Soble (1986) has suggested, the experience of masturbating to pornography may lead some men to question whether they are "man enough" to attract a real partner. Beneke (1990) notes that the *act of looking* at pornography distances men from women and that the stereotypic portrayals "defamiliarize" women to men. Furthermore, pornography manipulates men's sexuality: It provides misinformation about women's sexuality; teaches little, if anything, about affectionate contact, genuine intimacy, or feelings of vulnerability and uncertainty; and encourages men to believe that exerting power over women is desirable and fun for both women and men (Campbell 1990; Men Against Pornography 1990; Steinberg 1990). Rather than dissipating the anger engendered by men's perceptions of sexual scarcity, the pornographic myth of female availability may fuel angry feelings when real women do not conform to the images in pornography (Brod 1990). And as radical feminists have argued, pornography may help condition men's sexual response to women's powerlessness. By eroticizing male dominance and female submission in sexual relations, pornography makes sexism necessary for sexual arousal. Thus, according to John Stoltenberg (1989), while sex involving equality, mutuality, and tenderness fails to excite some men, injustice acted out sexually is a real turn-on.

Since pornography does not engage the emotions or spirit in any depth, ultimately it leaves the consumer unsatisfied (Kovel 1990). It also restricts male sensuality by placing primacy on the visual, narrowing the sexual experience "to such a degree that hearing, smell, [and] taste . . . have little to do with sexuality" (Guerrieri 1985, p. 9). The consumer eventually becomes oversaturated and bored with the unlimited exposure of body parts, leaving him less able "to be genuinely stimulated by human beings" and in need of more explicit, degrading, and violent imagery to get the same turn-on (Betzold 1977, p. 47; Men Against Pornography 1990).[11] Moreover, the objectification of women in pornography is directed back upon the male through his preoccupation with his penis and an overemphasis on genitals and orgasms as the sole basis of sexual satisfaction (Brod 1990; Litweka 1977; Tiefer 1987). Pornography socializes men to believe that sex revolves around technical expertise, and it promotes men's insecurity by putting pressure on them to perform flawlessly (Betzold 1977). Harry Brod (1990) believes that "male sexual . . . problems ranging from adolescent embarrassment at inopportune tumescence to impotence of various sorts can be traced . . . in part to pornographically induced obsessions with penile performance . . . [and] standards of sexual acrobatics performed by oversized organs" (pp. 198–9). Furthermore, pornography encourages men to control their feelings since emotion interferes with performance. Hence men become deadened to their feelings and "more powerless to meet their emotional needs" (Betzold 1977, p. 46). Kimmel (1990) adds that pornography may actually impoverish men's "sexual imaginations even in the guise of expanding our repertoires" (p. 318). The commercialization of sex narrows acceptable standards of beauty, making men less capable of developing their own standards of sexual attraction. According to Brod (1990), when both the diversity of desire and the humanity of desired objects are diminished, so is men's intensity of desire.

BLACK AND GAY MEN

Men have not been uniformly exposed to an invariant model of masculinity (Kimmel & Messner 1989). Race and sexual orientation are among the most important sources of variation, and both black men and gay men have spoken out on the issue of pornography.

Black Men

Like other men and women, black men who have written on pornography have expressed divergent points of view. Van White (1985) argues that pornography provides a poor model of education about sexuality and calls for men to take a strong stand against it, even though it may arouse them. He believes pornography's portrayal of women in submissive and animalistic roles degrades them and helps perpetuate their position as chattel.

White views women's treatment in pornography as reminiscent of blacks' experience with slavery, and laments that "many young women in search of a better life end up in the hands of pornographers" (p. 18). He asserts that pornography undermines the self-esteem of men as well as women, arguing that it is degrading for men to view women as lesser beings and thus to perpetuate "the same kind of hatred that brings racism to society."

Robert Staples (1990), on the other hand, conveys a rather hostile attitude toward the antipornography movement and calls pornography a "trivial issue" and "a white man's problem" (p. 111). He asserts that antipornography sentiments are a form of sexual prudery reflecting a white world-view that nonmarital sex is sinful. He argues that blacks have a more naturalistic view of sexuality than whites, and blames whites for trying to impose their sexual double standard on blacks. It was white missionaries, Staples says, who "forced African women to regard their quasi-nude bodies as sinful" (p. 112). He argues that antipornography activists want to keep women in "sexual straightjackets so that sexual pleasure remains a male domain," but that blacks believe that women have an equal right to sexual enjoyment (p. 113). He points out that blacks are overrepresented among those arrested for and convicted of rape, but argues that they consume relatively little pornography. This, he says, indicates that rape is more an expression of economic frustration than a result of pornography.

Gay Men

Gay men's writings focus on gay male pornography and reflect divergent views of it. For instance, Chris Clark (1985) sees gay pornography as an affirmation of gay sexuality that is particularly reassuring for those in the process of "coming out." For gay men, the fear of their own sexuality, and the "internalized self-hatred and self-disgust" this fear can entail, is the "most pernicious expression of sexism" (citing *Achilles Heel*, p. 15). Clark thus finds it hard not to agree that anything that helps undo the homophobic lessons of socialization and "that helps to free our repressed selves—including pornography—has a positive value." Since his entrance into the gay world was through a gay pornography establishment that offered pornographic films and nude dancing, Clark feels he cannot possibly take any position on pornography "other than *for* that which first affirmed and then later confirmed" his homosexuality (see Weinstein 1990). Nevertheless, the objectification, violence, and sexual power dynamics in much contemporary pornography lead Clark to have reservations about taking a pro-pornography position. Although he believes that sexual power is more predominant in heterosexual pornography than in gay pornography (because men and women are not gender equals),[12] he condemns the eroticization of power dynamics in all pornography and favors the development of "a pornography without power" that focuses on love relationships (p. 16).

Scott Tucker's (1990) defense of gay pornography is more strident and hostile toward antipornography feminism. He reiterates libertarian feminist arguments regarding the problems with radical feminist analyses and the liberating potential of pornography, and argues that pornography is a "positive part of gay male culture" (p. 269). He criticizes radical feminists for a "Bambi-Among-the-Buttercups-Utopianism," an unrealistic desire for a "homogenized humanity" where every person is always treated as a "whole person" (p. 265).

Stoltenberg (1985, 1989), on the other hand, offers an incisive critique of gay male pornography. He believes that pornography is not only harmful to women, but is a "major enforcer of cultural homophobia" (1989, p. 131). Stoltenberg argues that the source of homophobia is woman-hating and the positive valuation of gender polarity. Male supremacy, he says, rests on the derogation of female characteristics, and "the faggot is stigmatized because he is perceived to participate in the degraded status of the female" (1985, p. 46).[13] Homophobia protects "men from the sexual aggression of other men" and directs toward "women what [men] would not want done to themselves" (1989, p. 131). Stoltenberg adds that although gay male pornography often seems to portray "an idealized, all-male superbutch world," its frequent derogatory references to women and feminized males reinforce homophobia (1985, p. 46–47). According to Stoltenberg, several "codes" or conventions have been developed in gay male pornography that allow expression of "male sexual aggression and sadism" while also circumventing the stigmatization of men who are treated sexually like women. One code is the supermasculine portrayal of the "man who is 'capable' of withstanding 'discipline' "—for example, "punishing bondage, humiliation, and fistfucking" (1989, p. 132). Another code is the tendency to depict men "being ass-fucked . . . [as] ass-fucking someone else in turn . . . to avoid the connotation that he is . . . feminized by being fucked." Another is that scenes involving "mutuality are not sustained for very long without an intimation or explicit scene of force or coercion." Furthermore, Stoltenberg adds, the fetishization of the penis in gay pornography presents a rather narrow representation of sexuality: all that is shown is "the progress . . . [and] the status of the cock" (p. 249). The "hooking up [of] plumbing" is the only kind of connection portrayed.

Stoltenberg (1988) believes that the gay movement has made a serious mistake by not understanding the relationship between pornography and homophobia and by aligning itself economically and politically with pornographers. Economically, gay rights organizations have accepted money from the pornography industry. Politically, the gay community has defended the rights of pornographers on the false assumption that this defense would advance the cause of gay liberation. In the U.S. Supreme Court case of *Bowers v. Hardwick* (1986), gay rights activists supported an attack on antisodomy laws that was based on the right to privacy rather than on antidiscrimination arguments. In effect, the right to gay sex was "defended on the same grounds as the private possession of obscenity"[14] rather than on the grounds that antisodomy laws deny gays Fourteenth Amendment rights to equal protection under the law (Stoltenberg 1988, p. 12). If successful,[15] sodomy would have been shielded from prosecution only "in the most private of enclaves," and states could have continued to criminalize homosexual acts everywhere else (including, presumably, hotel rooms). Gay liberation, Stoltenberg argues, cannot occur while male supremacy and misogyny remain intact. As he says, "so long as the gay community defends the rights of pornographers to exploit and eroticize sex discrimination, . . . [gays] do not stand a chance" (p. 13).

CENSORSHIP, LIBERATION, AND RESPONSIBILITY

As we indicated above, many men do not experience their use of pornography as an expression of male power. They believe it has cathartic, educational, or affirmational value. Hence most men writing about pornography are opposed to censorship, which they believe would reinforce the view that sex is dirty and inherently dangerous and further state power to intrude upon individual sexual choice (Beneke 1990; Simon 1990; Steinberg 1990). Since pornography is seen more as "symptom than disease," censorship would detract from the real problem: eliminating sexism and violence against women (Small 1985, p. 7). Kimmel (1990) suggests that pornographic fantasies may draw on a reservoir of preexisting anger and resentment toward women and provide men with a culturally acceptable means of venting that rage. He says that it is men's anger at women, not pornography itself, that should be our primary concern, and that men's use of pornography is only one piece of a larger puzzle concerning the social construction of masculinity and femininity.

On the other hand, some men, though opposed to censorship, express dissatisfaction with civil libertarian views (feminist and nonfeminist) on pornography and sexual freedom. Alan Wolfe (1990) believes that "the case for censorship and the case for unrestricted rights to pornography are quite similar"; both lack "nuance" and neither understands the divided nature of the self (p. 30; see Randall 1989). Donald Downs (1989) feels that civil libertarians too readily dismiss as "misguided traditionalism" the need for a normative framework that establishes the moral grounds for an appropriate "human" sexuality (p. 177). Desire, he says, "does not operate outside social expectations and structures," and a normative framework is necessary for "defining ourselves as human" (p. 177). Most everyone, he maintains, finds sexual practices such as bestiality and necrophilia abhorrent, and most would agree with the contemporary prohibitions on adult-child sex. Downs endorses a vision of normative sexuality involving a "mutual respect between sexual equals [that] promotes the enlargement" of one another's spiritual selves. However, he acknowledges that some degree of objectification may be necessary for sexual arousal, and argues that primitive desire with its diminished personalization and its irrational and selfish character are also part of our nature. He agrees with Freud that "fully developed sexual relations" attempt to "reconcile the conflicting parts" of the self (Downs 1990, pp. 180–1).

According to Wolfe (1990), "we all have an interest in the many ways in which fundamental human conflicts are represented in print and film" (p. 31). To censor pornography, he believes, is to censor that part of ourselves that requires engagement or confrontation with the human condition. However, Wolfe acknowledges that most pornography retreats from this engagement. The "anything goes" or "diff'rent strokes for diff'rent folks" themes of pornography fail to address the tension between the different parts of the self. Joel Kovel (1990) goes even further, arguing the "pornographic" is distinguished from the "erotic" by its denial of the tensions inherent in human sexuality.

According to Brod (1990), sexual liberationists concerned about sexual repression have misconstrued sexual liberation to mean "any expression of sexuality" (p. 199). Those who believe that sex is natural and good and that pornography is intended to elicit sexual arousal often feel compelled to endorse pornography, "no matter how dreadful it may be" (Kovel 1990, p. 160). But this view underestimates pornography's role in reinforcing the very repressive sexual attitudes that it is apparently rebelling against. As Brod writes (1990), "To the extent that pornography's dehumanizing version of sexuality is accepted as valid, it lends credence to an antisexual morality. . . . Pornography flourishes in and is parasitic upon a repressive . . . sexual atmosphere" (p. 199).

Brod believes that pornography is ultimately anti-erotic. He argues that truly "erotic arousal arises from the union achieved" in overcoming the distance between the "desired object" and the "desiring subject" (pp. 194–5). "Eros" does not seek to reduce the tension, but rather to prolong the desiring, to bask in the shared pleasure, to create "new dimensions of experience which broaden the being of both persons" (citing Rollo May, p. 195).[16] In conventional pornography, "the body is reduced to an object, and no personality shows through. In erotica, the personality is expressed through the body as the subjective agent behind the sexual self. . . . Whereas erotica unites and expands relations between the self and others, . . . pornography isolates and constricts" (p. 196). But, Brod argues, many men resist "eros," viewing "relational affection" and sensuality as unwanted intrusions into their sexual experiences.

Stoltenberg (1989), a supporter of the Dworkin-MacKinnon civil rights approach, adds that the struggle against sexual repression has been primarily a struggle for men to produce and consume whatever *they* wished. "Sexual freedom has been about preserving a sexuality that preserves male supremacy" (p. 127). Sexual freedom has not meant sexual self-determination or sexual justice and equality between women and men. Although "pornography tells lies about women," Stoltenberg maintains, it "tells the truth about men" (p. 121):

It is almost as if the pornography industry and its defenders are truly embarrassed to admit that some of the stuff they turn out could conceivably excite some man somewhere to sexual arousal. So pornography is defended as 'speech,' as 'art,' as the working of a free press, as the product of free enterprise, as the symbol of a free society, as 'liberated' sex—meanwhile what is left unsaid is . . . that what sells sells because it creates and feeds men's sexual appetites. All pornography exists because it connects to some man's sexuality somewhere. (pp. 120–1)

Without sexual justice, Stoltenberg argues, it is not possible to achieve true sexual freedom. Men, he says, have a responsibility to confront pornography's eroticization of dominance and submission. Men must talk to each other about what's being done "in our names as men, as entertainment for men, for the sake of some delusion of so-called manhood" (p. 135). It will not do to simply say that pornography, sexual fantasies, and fantasies of male power have no relationship to sexual attitudes and conduct (Campbell 1990). "Each consumer, each purchaser of a reproduced documentation of the original sexual objectification, is complicitous in the commerce, a link in the chain of profit, and hence he bears some responsibility, however widely shared by others, for the act of sexual objectification that took place in front of the camera" (Stoltenberg 1989, p. 49). Stoltenberg believes that part of the pleasure men receive looking at pornography involves the knowledge that they share this experience with other men. Men must confront this implicit bonding with other men that takes place when men view pornography together (see Di Lauro & Rabkin 1976). Phenomena such as gang rape (including fraternity rape), the telling of sexist jokes, and the general bravado with which men boast to one another about their sexual conquests must also be challenged by men, not just by women (see Brod 1990; Chancer 1987; Lyman 1987; Martin & Hummer 1989).

CONCLUSION

Kimmel (1990) calls for men to confront the issue of pornography and analyze the role of sexuality "both as a cornerstone of male supremacy and, in its liberatory capacity, as one of the chief weapons we may have to assist in the dismantling of gender inequality and in the creation of a world in which we all—women and men, gay and straight—can be equal in desire" (p. 22). Such an effort does not require men to deny sexual pleasure or fantasies, but rather to listen to what women have to say about sexuality, pornography, and victimization; to acknowledge one's sexual feelings and explore means to self-empowerment; to create arousing but nonabusive sexual imagery;[17] to talk to men about sexuality and make alliances with them "in open defiance of both sexual repression and sexist violence, and in loving support of a common struggle within and against a repressive culture" (p. 319). Small (1985) adds that "nearly all of us . . . are survivors of deep hurt and humiliation around sexuality and nudity, . . . [and] we need to think about and heal the hurts in our lives that have left us with sexual compulsions, addictions, and obsessions (pp. 43, 45).

Wolfe (1990), however, urges us to confront the legal implications of the pornography debate, a subject we will take up in Chapter 7 of this book. He believes we need to develop a legal standard capable of balancing the needs served by pornography with the problems it entails. As he says,

Since pornography is part of what we are, we harm ourselves by regulating it too severely. . . . [But] the age of AIDS should teach us . . . [that society] cannot take a position of . . . [complete] neutrality toward the libido. . . . So long as tax monies are used to save lives, there *is* a public interest in private sex. . . . Some sexual freedom is . . . necessary to discover the self. Some regulation is . . . necessary to protect the society without which there can be no selves. (p. 30–31)

NOTES

1. For a discussion of historical parallels, see Kimmel (1987a, 1987c).

2. We discussed Soble in Chapter 4 because his work is offered as an explicit attempt to develop a Marxist analysis of pornography rather than a men's perspective per se.

3. Men also resent women because they have learned to depend upon women to help them express their emotions, and even to express "their emotions for them" (Pleck 1989, p. 23).

4. Kimmel also argues that not only do many men feel vulnerable to sexual rejection by women, but they also feel powerless, even

"feminized," in the workplace. Pornographic fantasy can thus be seen "as revenge against the real world of men's lives" (p. 315).

5. These writings are embedded in a theoretical tradition that views men's desire to achieve dominance over women as "a lifelong psychological need to free themselves from or prevent their dominance by women," a need that is rooted in males' early experiences with mothers and elementary school teachers. "Men oppress women as adults because they experienced women as oppressing them as children" (Pleck 1989, p. 22).

6. Beneke notes that women experimenting with a "pleasure model of sex" (for example, as advocated by libertarian feminists) may be attempting to overcome the traditional "madonna" image of womanhood (p. 183). But while sexually explicit imagery may be a vehicle for overcoming traditional restrictions on female sexuality, Beneke believes that most men will have great difficulty viewing women seeking sexual liberation as anything other than "whores." Any commercial image that represents women's sexuality, even in a nonsexist manner, will encourage some men to view female sexuality as a commodity "to be bought, sold, gotten for free, or stolen" (p. 186).

7. According to Beneke, the problem is not that pornography turns women into objects, but that it turns them into "narrowly subjectified bodies" (p. 177). Common stereotyped subjectivities conveyed in pornography include women as alluring, lusty, coy, compliant, etc.

8. Mura sees the pornography addict as a victim of sexual, physical, and/or emotional abuse, one who has been conditioned to take "the act of abuse for love, for the standard of sexuality" (p. 19). Only recently has the concept of sexual addiction, previously limited to conservative discourse and psychological literature, been given serious consideration by feminists (Herman 1988).

9. Both Warren Farrell and Bob Guccione (publisher of *Penthouse*) made this point on a television interview program ("Larry King Live," CNN, April 4, 1987).

10. Pornography may also alienate women from men by stereotyping men as sexual aggressors, thereby heightening women's distrust of men (Campbell 1990).

11. Brod (1987) notes that "as one moves from soft to hardcore pornography, the average age of the male consumer increases from adolescence to midlife." He asks whether this is due merely to

overexposure and the consequent "need for greater doses to reach satisfaction," or whether other factors "relating to the waxing and waning of the power of both the physical and social self" are involved (p. 16–17).

12. Clark argues that refuting "this distinction between gay and straight porn is itself homophobic; since gay men begin as gender-equals" (p. 16). He says that "the only way to conflate gay and straight porn is to label one participant as the passive-feminine role." Stoltenberg (1990), on the other hand, maintains that gay men often treat each other "like a woman" during sexual interactions.

13. Stoltenberg (1990) adds that the lesbian is derogated not only because she is a woman, but also because she has the "gall not to flatter the phallic ego" (p. 250).

14. See the discussion of *Stanley v. Georgia* (1969) in Chapter 7.

15. In *Hardwick* the court ruled that antisodomy laws were constitutional.

16. In contrast to "eros," "thanatos," the death instinct, represents the cessation of desire. Brod describes pornography as thanatic because it aims to extinguish desire.

17. Small (1985) calls for taking "the best of the pornographic tradition—sexual openness, exploration, and celebration—and add[ing] egalitarian values, imagination, artfulness, respect for ourselves, and respect for the power and beauty of sex itself" (p. 43).

6

The Research Context
of the Feminist Debate

As we indicated in Chapter 1, a social constructionist approach
defines social problems as the product of "activities of individuals
or groups making assertions of grievances and claims with respect
to some putative condition" (Spector & Kitsuse 1977, p. 75). The
process by which these claims are successfully advanced depends
in part on their grounding in empirical evidence.[1] Thus far we
have considered competing claims about pornography made by
a variety of feminist perspectives. In this chapter we examine
the empirical social science evidence that has become part of the
grounds upon which the various sides of the debate base their
claims. As is often the case in any research tradition, the basic
facts that establish the grounds for claims are much in dispute. For
instance, in Chapter 2 we noted controversies over the 1970 and
1986 pornography commissions' use of social science evidence
to buttress their positions.

The pornography literature is replete with different interpretations of the research evidence, including reviews by feminists
who interpret the findings as definitive proof of harm (Bart 1985)
and as proof of no harm (McCormack 1985b). Complicating

the issue is the possibility that audiences (for example, the general public or political officials) exposed to this information may accept a particular interpretation of the evidence without necessarily adopting the associated policy recommendations. "Policy making is as much an expression of values, . . . interests, . . . [and] intuition, as it is an interpretation of social science" (Einsiedel 1989, p. 96).

Social scientists generally adhere to positivist approaches embedded in liberal epistemology (see Chapter 4). Thus they often make claims to expertise and value neutrality when investigating an issue. Indeed, their very designation as "scientists" implies superiority of their methods over nonscientific methods of investigation. By employing "objective" methods for studying social problems, social scientists claim to draw conclusions about social problems that are superior to or more rational than those based on rectitude—that is, assertions about appropriate values or views of morality (see Best 1987). Yet scientific activity itself may be viewed as a social construction—that is, a process by which some versions of reality come to predominate over others (see Gieryn 1983).

In this chapter, we review the social science evidence regarding pornography and some of the problems associated with this research tradition. This review is not meant to be exhaustive (see Donnerstein et al. 1987; Hawkins & Zimring 1988; Osanka & Johann 1989). Rather, we emphasize what we believe to be the most significant findings that bear upon conclusions drawn by feminists in the pornography debate. In the following sections we consider studies that assess the quantity and quality (type) of available pornography, the correlation between pornography and rape, and the experimental effects of exposure to pornography. It is difficult to draw definitive conclusions from the research because one cannot assume that the operational definition of terms is consistent across all studies or that it matches either feminist theorists' or laypeoples' conceptions (see Gillespie & Leffler 1987). For example, some researchers utilize a more narrow definition of violence than others. Is the sexual coercion of a less powerful person by a more powerful person an indication of "violence"? Not necessarily, in the research reviewed below.[2]

THE QUANTITY AND QUALITY OF PORNOGRAPHY

Antipornography feminists have claimed that in the last two decades a greater proportion of the available pornography has become violent and the degree of violence portrayed has become more extreme. The Attorney General's Commission (1986) concurred with this assessment, asserting that violent pornography was "the most prevalent" form (p. 323). Anticensorship forces, both feminist and nonfeminist, believe such claims to be exaggerated.[3]

There are a number of "content analysis" studies that shed some light on this issue. In these studies, researchers attempt to document the quantity or quality of particular materials or subject matter available during a certain time period. For instance, Donald Smith (1976) found that both sexual explicitness and depictions of rape (typically with no adverse consequences to the aggressor) increased in "adults only" paperback novels between 1968 and 1974, and that rape depictions were prevalent in about one third of the sex scenes. Similarly, Neil Malamuth and Barry Spinner (1980) observed that violent images in *Playboy* and *Penthouse* magazines increased from one percent in 1973 to five percent in 1977. However, by the early 1980s, studies indicated that the violent imagery in *Playboy* had decreased since its peak in 1977, possibly in response to the Malamuth and Spinner research (Malamuth 1985; Scott 1986; Scott & Cuvelier 1987). Although the mass circulation of top-selling sexually explicit magazines decreased from the mid-1970s to mid-1980s (Attorney General's Commission 1986), Park Dietz and Barbara Evans (1982) found that themes of bondage and domination were depicted on about 17 percent of adult sex magazine covers. On detective magazine covers, Dietz, Bruce Harry, and Robert Hazelwood (1986) found bondage themes on 76 percent and domination themes on 38 percent.

As for films, Joseph Slade (1984) found that on the average only five percent of pornographic stag films between 1915 and 1972 contained rape, although the violence had become more graphic and brutal since 1970. According to Stephen Prince (1987), the incidence of rape in top-selling pornographic films decreased from about 33 percent between 1976 and 1979 to about seven percent by 1980–85. T. S. Palys' (1986) study of videos between 1979 and 1983 revealed that "adult" videos (containing nudity and implied or nonexplicit sex[4]) depicted more male dominance and aggression than X-rated videos.

The content analysis research seems to support libertarian feminists' contention that a substantial portion of contemporary pornography is not especially violent, at least if a narrow definition is employed. Nevertheless, Edward Donnerstein, Daniel Linz, and Steven Penrod (1987) concluded "that the sheer quantity of violent and nonviolent pornographic materials that are for sale or rent in the United States has increased" since the early 1970s (p. 91; see Scott 1985). They also concurred with Palys's (1986) observation about the contemporary video market: "[If] our concern is with violence and sexual violence, . . . our attention . . . would be better directed to what is on the shelves [R-rated films that include sex and violence] rather than what is under the counter" (p. 33). Indeed, the Attorney General's Commission (1986) reported that R-rated films comprised about 45 percent of available films, while X-rated films comprised about five percent. Similarly, Gordon Hawkins and Franklin Zimring (1988) noted that the most important development in recent years has been the "integration of sexually explicit communications into the mainstream of the American communications industry . . . [and] mainstream channels of commerce" (p. 70). Sex magazines are more readily available at the corner newsstand than at adult bookstores or through mail-order sources, and violent and sexually explicit videos are more available at neighborhood rental outlets than at peep-show houses or adult theatres.

CORRELATIONAL STUDIES

Correlational studies examine whether there is a statistical association between rates of rape and the availability of pornography.
Some correlational research has also examined the relationship
between rape and the legal status of pornography. In one of the
earliest studies, Berl Kutchinsky (1973) noted a downward trend
in sex crimes following the repeal of antipornography laws in
Denmark. However, John Court (1976, 1984) argued that the
decrease stemmed from the decriminalization of various sex
offenses, and that rates of rape actually increased in Denmark
and other countries and cities that legalized pornography. Later,
Kutchinsky (1985) responded that the increase in rape rates in
Denmark occurred while the production and consumption of
pornography decreased. Others noted that Court did not present
data on the consumption of pornography, and that his data from
some of the localities studied did not support his contention that
antipornography laws reduced rape or that legalization increased
rape (Donnerstein et al. 1987). Thus, the evidence does not
warrant any definitive conclusion about the relationship between
rape and the criminalization/legalization of pornography.

In one of the most important correlational studies to date,
Larry Baron and Murray Straus (1987, 1989), using state-by-
state data from the fifty states in the United States, found
a positive association between rape rates and sex magazine
circulation rates (based on subscription and newsstand sales of
eight magazines—*Chic, Club, Gallery, Genesis, Hustler, Oui,
Penthouse*, and *Playboy*). This association was apparent while
controlling for other factors including gender equality, social
disorganization, and general cultural support for violence.[5] However, Baron and Straus argued that the association between
sex magazines and rape was due to another yet-unmeasured
factor—"hypermasculinity." They based this view on studies
that found an association between rape and "macho" cultural
patterns (McCarthy 1980; Mosher & Anderson 1986; Sanday
1981). However, their cultural support for violence measure

(which might be associated with hypermasculinity) exhibited no direct association with rape.[6]

In support of Baron and Straus's skepticism regarding the relationship between pornography and rape, Joseph Scott and Loretta Schwalm (1988a) found no association between rape rates and the availability of adult theatres. On the other hand, they did find an association between rape and outdoor magazine circulation rates (based on *American Rifleman*, *Field and Stream*, *Guns and Ammo*, *Sports Afield*, and *The American Hunter*), which might be interpreted as lending support to Baron and Straus's contention about hypermasculinity. These results, however, should be read with caution. Adult theatres (since the advent of the video market) are not good indicators of the availability of pornography. Moreover, because of lack of data, Scott and Schwalm were forced to lump various states together, leaving them with only forty-one areas for their statistical analysis. In addition, Scott and Schwalm (1988b) published another study which did find a statistically significant relationship between rape and sex magazine circulation rates, even when controlling for outdoor magazine circulation rates.

Thus while Baron and Straus were inclined to disregard their own results, the association between sex magazine circulation and rape is "difficult to dismiss out of hand" (Einsiedel 1989, p. 93). Indeed, the sex magazine index was one of the best predictors of rape rates in their study. It is likely that researchers less interested than Baron and Straus in discounting a link between pornography and rape would have interpreted the results differently.

EXPERIMENTAL EVIDENCE

According to social psychologists, the advantage of the experimental method is the controlled laboratory setting that allows "the unambiguous assignment of causality," where the "researcher is justified in making a strong statement concerning the relationship of factor A to factor B" (Donnerstein et al. 1987, p. 10). In an experiment subjects are randomly assigned to experimental treatments or conditions (including a control group) and their responses to differential treatments are compared. The experiments on pornography have examined various types of violent and nonviolent sexually explicit materials: subjects have read or listened to vignettes and stories and have viewed slides, photographs, scenes from films, stag films, and feature-length films (X-rated and R-rated). The effects of these materials have been measured through studies of sexual arousal (penile tumescence), changes in perception and attitudes (regarding sexual violence and women), and laboratory aggression (administration of electric shock or aversive noise). The variety of experimental designs makes it very difficult to draw general conclusions about pornography and leaves much room for different interpretations of the results.

Male Subjects' Reactions

Perhaps the most consistent findings of the experimental research come from studies that examine male subjects' reactions to aggressive or violent pornography, generally defined by experimental researchers as depictions involving sexual coercion or force (Malamuth 1985). One important finding concerns the effect of predisposition to sexual aggression on subjects' responses to experimental exposure. Subjects who were more predisposed to sexual aggression—that is, those who reported they would be likely to rape if they thought they would not be caught or punished, those who exhibited higher levels of sexual arousal to depictions of rape than to depictions of consensual sex, and those who harbored relatively high levels of anger toward women—were influenced to a greater degree than subjects who were less predisposed to aggression (Donnerstein et al. 1987; Gray 1982; Malamuth 1985). Such differences have led some to conclude that the effects of exposure are entirely "consistent with the subject's usual practices" (McCormack 1985b, p. 188) and do not *cause* predispositions to violence but rather "reinforce and strengthen already existing beliefs and values" (Donnerstein & Linz 1986a,

p. 58). These results caution against overgeneralizing about the effects of pornography on men.

Another significant finding that cuts across much of the research on aggressive pornography concerns the critical importance of the portrayal of victim reactions to sexual aggression. Experimental exposure had the greatest effect when the pornography portrayed women as enjoying sexual coercion. For example, when victims were portrayed as abhorring sexual assault (referred to as "negative" victim reaction), male subjects indicated relatively little sexual arousal to rape scenes; but when victims were portrayed as becoming involuntarily aroused (referred to as "positive" victim reaction), subjects' sexual arousal to rape scenes was as high as to portrayals of consensual sex (Malamuth & Check 1980a, 1980b; Malamuth et al. 1980). However, males who indicated a likelihood of raping if they would not get caught showed more sexual arousal to rape depictions than to consensual sex regardless of victims' reactions (Malamuth 1981a, 1981b, 1984). These males resembled rapists in the way they responded to aggressive pornography.

Studies of the effects of aggressive pornography on subjects' perceptions and attitudes yielded similar results, as did studies of nonexplicit films with scenes of sexual violence (for example, *The Getaway* and *Swept Away*). When compared to male subjects exposed to material involving either "negative" victim reactions or consensual sex, male subjects exposed to material involving "positive" victim reactions reported less sensitivity to rape victims as well as an increase in rape fantasies, in the self-reported possibility of committing rape, and in acceptance of rape myths and interpersonal violence against women (Donnerstein & Berkowitz 1981; Donnerstein & Linz 1986a; Malamuth 1981b; Malamuth & Check 1981, 1985).

Conclusions from laboratory aggression studies are particularly difficult to draw due to the diversity of experimental designs. The findings of these studies have differed according to whether it was a male or female confederate of the experimenter who predisposed the subject to aggression by angering him (for example, by insulting him or giving him an electric shock), whether the target of the aggression was a male or female, and whether the subject was given multiple opportunities to aggress against the target. However, the most significant findings were that aggressive pornographic depictions, more than nonpornographic aggressive depictions (for example, a man hitting a woman), increased laboratory aggression toward women, and that nonpornographic aggressive material, more than nonaggressive pornographic material (for example, consensual sex) increased aggression toward women (Donnerstein 1980, 1984; Donnerstein & Berkowitz 1981; Malamuth 1983, 1984). Additionally, there were no differences found between sex-only films and "neutral content" (no sex or violence) films (Donnerstein et al. 1986), and there was evidence that some nonaggressive pornography (for example, materials perceived as mildly erotic, such as pictures from *Playboy*) actually reduced laboratory aggression (Donnerstein et al. 1975; Zillmann et al. 1981). However, aggressive pornography with "positive" victim reactions increased aggression for both experimentally angered and nonangered subjects, while aggressive pornography with "negative" victim reactions increased aggression for only angered subjects. Neil Malamuth (1985) concludes that "negative" victim reactions appear to inhibit aggression in nonangered subjects only, while "positive" victim reactions appear to justify aggression and reduce inhibitions in both angered and nonangered subjects.

In an attempt to demonstrate that it is violence, not sex, that has the most harmful effects, Donnerstein et al. (1986) exposed subjects to scenes from three edited versions of the same film: one containing "sexual aggression in which a woman was tied up, threatened with a gun, and raped"; one containing "only the violent parts of the scene, with the sexually explicit rape removed"; and one containing "the sexually explicit parts of the scene, with most of violence deleted" (see Donnerstein et al. 1987, p. 110). The highest levels of laboratory aggression were found in the sex-with-violence version, while the lowest levels were found in the sex-only version. Moreover, subjects seeing the violence-only version actually displayed the most calloused attitudes about rape and were the most likely to indicate they might rape or use force against women. On the other hand, subjects viewing the sex-only film displayed the least calloused attitudes and were the least likely to indicate they might rape.

Donnerstein et al. (1987) conclude that "violence against women need not occur in a pornographic or sexually explicit context to have a negative effect on viewer attitudes and behavior" (p. 112). Among the diversity of films available in the marketplace, they believe that R-rated movies which contain eroticized violence are the most troublesome. They studied the effects of so-called "slasher" films such as *Texas Chainsaw Massacre, Maniac, I Spit on Your Grave, Vice Squad,* and *Toolbox Murders* (see Linz et al. 1984). These films typically have female victims and contain explicitly violent scenes that are often juxtaposed with erotic scenes. In experiments using these films, college male subjects were screened for any predisposition toward aggression, as indicated by their scores on a psychological inventory measuring hostility and psychoticism. Students so predisposed were removed from the study and the remaining psychologically "normal" subjects were exposed to the R-rated movies over a period of five days. Donnerstein et al. found that these subjects became desensitized to the violence: they reported seeing fewer violent and offensive scenes, and they rated the films less graphic, gory, and degrading to women, as well as more enjoyable and entertaining. After viewing a videotaped reenactment of a rape trial, these subjects, compared to a control group that had not seen the films, had less sympathy for the rape victim and perceived her as a less worthy and attractive individual. They also judged the defendant less responsible for the rape and thought the victim offered less resistance and received less injury. In a replication of this experiment, Linz (1985) found that two movies (lasting about three hours and containing twenty to twenty-five violent acts) were sufficient to obtain these effects.

In comparison to research on aggressive pornography and on R-rated films with sexually violent themes, the experimental evidence on the effects of nonviolent or nonaggressive porno-graphy has been less conclusive (Donnerstein et al. 1987). Don-nerstein and associates have been the leading proponents of the view that the research demonstrates that this material is not harmful, while Dolf Zillmann and Jennings Bryant have expressed the opposite view. Zillmann and Bryant (1982, 1984) exposed male subjects to nearly five hours of nonviolent pornographic scenes over a six-week period. These subjects reported increased callousness toward women (as indicated by agreement with statements like "A man should find them, feel them, fuck them, and forget them"), decreased support of women's equality, and increased leniency (less punishment) for rapists.

In contrast to Zillmann and Bryant, Linz (1985) did not find adverse experimental effects from about eight hours' exposure (over a two-week period) to feature-length, nonviolent X-rated films such as *Debbie Does Dallas*. While the shorter-term expo-sure may have been insufficient to change viewer attitudes, the differing results may be due to the varying content of the materials. Zillmann and Bryant exposed subjects to unconnected pornographic scenes that degraded women and portrayed them as sexually promiscuous and insatiable. Linz used materials that were more plot-oriented, albeit "predictable and sophomoric" (Linz et al. 1988, p. 767). These films often took place in scenic locations and the women were portrayed in everyday "activities such as traveling in cars, eating in restaurants, going to movies, . . . and so forth." Linz et al. argued that the inclusion of these images in the films may have competed with or interfered with viewers' perceptions of female promiscuity and insatiability.

In a subsequent stage of their research, Zillmann and Bryant (1986) gave their male subjects an opportunity to later view other media, including various forms of pornography. These subjects tended to choose the more violent materials that included bondage, sadomasochism, and bestiality. However, while sub-jects' appetites for these materials may have been stimulated by the earlier exposure, there was no evidence of lasting changes in tastes. In the context of the experiment, subjects may have merely become bored or curious (Donnerstein et al. 1987). Moreover, experimental exposure to the initial nonviolent pornography did not increase subjects' laboratory aggression.

In addition, Zillmann and Bryant (1986) found that male subjects exposed to nonviolent pornographic films, in comparison to a control group, reported less satisfaction with their mate's physical appearance and sexual performance, and thought more positively about recreational sex without emotional involvement. Similar results have been obtained with exposure to *Playboy* and *Penthouse* magazines and to television programs and magazine ads that portray conventionally attractive women (Donnerstein et al. 1987; Kenrick & Gutierres 1980). These latter findings indicate that it is not only pornography that influences men's perceptions of women, but also other images of women that pervade popular media (Steele 1985). However, not all studies indicate that the influences are negative. For example, Marshall Dermer and Thomas Pyszczynski (1978) found that reading erotic passages from adult magazines increased subjects' scores on a psychological inventory measuring attachment, caring, and intimacy for mates. In addition, pornography has been used in clinical settings with positive results for persons with sexual dysfunctions or unsatisfactory sex lives (Wilson 1978).

Female Subjects' Reactions

In comparison to experimental studies with males, there have been few studies with female subjects. Robert Baron (1979) found that pictures of nonpornographic art and scenery, men in bathing suits, male nudes from *Playgirl* magazine, and couples engaged in sexual acts did not increase the laboratory aggression of nonangered women, whereas the pictures of sexual acts did increase the aggression of angered women. According to Zillman and Bryant (1982, 1984), females' exposure to nonaggressive pornography increased callousness toward women, decreased support for women's equality, and increased lenient attitudes toward rapists. However, Carol Krafka (1985) found no adverse experimental effects on females' perceptions and attitudes from the nonviolent X-rated films used by Linz (1985), although she did find that female viewers became sexually aroused to depictions of rape with "positive" victim reactions.

Krafka (1985) also studied the effects on females of experimental exposure to the R-rated films with eroticized violence used by Donnerstein and associates (1987; Linz et al. 1984). Although female viewers did not report seeing less violence following initial exposure, they did experience some desensitization (that is, a reduction in anxiety and depression). In addition, their judgments about rape victims (as measured by their reactions to the videotaped reenactments of a rape trial) were negatively affected. Krafka hypothesized that the female viewers engaged in self-protective reactions that allowed them to disassociate themselves from the violence by holding other women responsible for their own victimization. On the other hand, Malamuth and James Check (1981) found that aggressive pornography actually increased female viewers' sensitivity to rape victims—that is, it decreased their acceptance of rape myths and interpersonal violence against women.

Finally, some research suggests that males and females may reinforce each others perceptions of sexually violent films. For instance, Zillman, James Weaver, Norbert Mundorf, and Charles Aust (1986) found that male viewers enjoyed R-rated "slasher" films more when accompanied by female companions who were distressed by the violence, while female viewers enjoyed the films more (and found their male companions more attractive) when the male displayed a "macho" attitude toward the violence.[7]

Mitigating the Effects of Pornography

In addition to studies of the effects of pornography, experimental research has examined potential ways to mitigate the effects of pornography. Several studies have examined the effects on male and female subjects of various postexperimental *debriefings* intended to counter negative media imagery. After exposing subjects to various stories of rape, Malamuth and Check (1984) presented subjects with two types of debriefings: one involving a general discussion of the benefits of human sexuality research, and one specifically designed to counter belief in rape myths. Subjects exposed to the latter were less inclined to believe in rape myths. Other studies found that exposure to depictions of rape reduced belief in rape myths when countered by a debriefing that debunked rape myths (Malamuth & Check 1980b, 1984; Malamuth et al. 1980). Linz (1985) and Krafka (1985) found that debriefings tailored to nonviolent R-rated, nonviolent X-rated, and violent R-rated films reduced belief in rape myths, especially for the violent films.

Studies of pre-film *briefings* have produced mixed results. Short briefings similar to cigarette warnings that inform subjects about the potential impact of aggressive pornography on viewer attitudes and behavior had little influence on viewers' perceptions or attitudes (Bross 1984). However, longer briefings using video-taped messages were effective in reducing belief in rape myths. Briefings involving general matters regarding sexual relationships (including sexual responsibility) and those focusing specifically on rape proved equally effective (Intons-Peterson & Roskos-Ewoldsen 1989). Margaret Intons-Peterson and Beverly Roskos-Ewoldsen (1989) argue that such briefings not only "sensitize people to rape myths and make them less susceptible to the callousing effects of violent pornography," but also educate about sexuality and interpersonal relationships (p. 234). These "mitigating effects" studies underscore the value of sex education, which other research has found to be associated with reductions in sexual assault and abuse, as well as unwanted pregnancies and abortions (Furstenberg et al. 1985; Jones et al. 1985; Zabin et al. 1986).

Criticisms of Experimental Research

At the beginning of this chapter we noted that researchers differ in their assessment of pornography research. Malamuth (1985) interprets the experimental evidence as strongly supporting the view that at least some pornography contributes "to a cultural climate that is more accepting of aggression against women" (p. 405). On the other hand, Alexis Durham (1986) believes this research has "no currently demonstrable relationship to real world behavior" (p. 102), and Thelma McCormack asserts that "there is no systematic evidence to link either directly or indirectly the use of pornography . . . with rape" and that the results are not "strong enough to support any social policy" recommendations (1985b, p. 202; 1985a, p. 279).

Other observers question the behavioristic assumptions underlying this research, which treat human sexual response as if it were "a reflex action unmediated by social categories," and criticize experimenters for not examining the way pornographic materials are interpreted and rendered meaningful by individuals (Ashley & Ashley 1984, p. 357). McCormack (1985b) argues that if consensual sexual depictions induce negative attitudes toward women, then the problem is not the sexual depictions themselves, but the way "men interpret their own sexual arousal and what it means to them" (p. 195). McCormack is also concerned that studies of sexual arousal may be biased because the apparatus used to measure penile tumescence may itself stimulate sexual arousal and because subjects' self-reports of sexual arousal may be unreliable. Other critics note that laboratory aggression is a poor measure of real-life aggression, and that subjects may feel they have been given permission by the researcher to aggress in the experiment (Downs 1989). In addition, the generalizability of the research is limited since virtually all the experiments have been conducted with undergraduate college students. David Sears (1986) notes that this age group (usually eighteen to twenty-two years old), in comparison to older adults, has more mutable attitudes, is more prone to attitude-behavior inconsistency, and is less self-reflective about their attitudes and behavior.

Although radical feminists and other antipornography activists use the experimental research to support their claims about the harm of pornography, their view that pornography is harmful is not dependent upon this research. Radical feminist epistemology, as we noted earlier, takes "women's standpoint" as the basis for knowledge and finds knowledge derived from women's personal experience more valid. Radical feminists are critical of the fact that the experimental research, generally involving males studying males, has higher prestige than the evidence of harm taken from the testimony of victims of pornography or contained in the pictures of abuse itself (Dworkin 1984; MacKinnon 1986).[8] Experimental research also has higher prestige than social science surveys that reveal women's negative experiences with pornography and than clinical evidence provided by professionals (for example, therapists, district attorneys) who work with victims or with convicted and self-reported sex offenders (see Chapter 3). While the experimenters say they cannot determine whether pornography *causes* rape, and some critics question laboratory studies for their artificiality and lack of correspondence to the real world, radical feminists complain that the testimony of "real women, men and children who have been abused because of pornography" is discounted and dismissed as merely anecdotal (Bart 1986, p. 105). Harry Brod (1990) adds that the experimental research only measures whether *increased* exposure leads to *increased* "pro-violent attitudes or behaviors above what is considered a societal norm" (p. 197). The research does not measure "the effect of the general circulation of pornography in establishing a norm of dominating and exploitative sexuality throughout the culture."

CONCLUSION

Irrespective of social science research findings, antipornography feminists assert that some forms of pornography are inherently objectionable (Clark 1983). For example, Helen Longino (1980) finds pornography immoral because, by definition, it "represents or describes sexual behavior that is degrading or abusive to one or more of the participants *in such a way as to endorse the degradation*" (p. 43). Similarly, Judith DeCew

(1984) believes that one can unconditionally conclude that all violent pornography is, by the very nature of the case, morally wrong because it "approvingly depicts" nonconsensual, coercive, or abusive treatment of human beings in a way that fails to respect their dignity and worth (p. 92). Thus she argues that it is not necessary to make the immorality of violent pornography conditional upon the empirical demonstration of harmful consequences. However, such presumptive assertions have generally fallen short in convincing anticensorship forces as well as many neutral and undecided observers that pornography causes sufficient harm to justify legal remedies. They believe that the evidence of harm is too weak to justify restrictions on civil liberties.

Some observers suggest that educational strategies based on experimental evidence regarding ways to mitigate the effects of pornography would have greater potential to attract a broader base of support among feminists (Einsiedel 1989; Intons-Peterson & Roskos-Ewoldsen 1989). They generally envision prebriefing and debriefing messages as part of more comprehensive educational interventions about gender roles, interpersonal relationships, sexuality, sexual responsibility, and critical media viewing. These nonlegal educational approaches are also the strategies recommended by the leading social science researchers (Donnerstein et al. 1987; Malamuth 1985; see Chapter 8).

NOTES

1. For a more general theoretical discussion of how grounds are used in claims-making activities, see Joel Best (1987).

2. For example, Margaret Intons-Peterson and Beverly Roskos-Ewoldsen (1989) distinguish coercion from aggression. They label the former "pornography" and the latter "violent pornography."

3. An additional concern has been child pornography. Since the U.S. Supreme Court decision of *New York v. Ferber* (1982), which allowed prohibition of child pornography, there has been a virtual consensus that child pornography should be banned. Shirley O'Brien (1983) estimates that child pornography comprised about five to ten

percent of the pornography trade in the late 1970s. However, since 1980 this trade has been illegal in virtually every country, and most child pornography is now produced by child abusers themselves in "cottage industry" fashion (Attorney General's Commission 1986). According to Berl Kutchinsky (1983), consumers of child pornography constitute a small "outcast sexual minority" (p. 1081). Hawkins and Zimring (1988) add that public concerns about the effects of child pornography should also address films that use young adult actors depicted as children.

4. Palys studied videos available in British Columbia, Canada. These would receive an R rating in the U.S.

5. Baron and Straus constructed a "legitimate violence index" that included several indicators that measured factors such as violent magazine circulation, violent television viewing, death penalty utilization, National Guard expenditures, and hunting licenses sold.

6. The cultural support for violence measure was indirectly related to rape through its (negative) influence on gender equality. Baron and Straus argued that legitimized violence lowered gender equality, which in turn increased rape.

Baron and Straus also examined the effects of an additional indicator to measure hypermasculinity. They constructed a "violence approval index" based on questions from the General Social Survey that asked respondents about their attitudes toward the use of violence and force. (This indicator was correlated with the "legitimate violence index.") When used in the multiple regression analysis, the "violence approval index" eliminated the independent effect of the sex magazine index, but was not related to rape. Regardless, Baron and Straus acknowledge that this measure may be unreliable. The General Social Survey is designed as a national and regional sample and does not randomly sample by state. Since sufficient numbers of respondents were not available for every state, their analysis was conducted with only 40 states.

7. Edward Sadella, Douglas Kenrick, and Beth Vershure (1987) found that females were more attracted to males who displayed dominance characteristics.

8. Andrea Dworkin (1984) also points to the use of pornography to desensitize medical students to human pain and the use of pornography by the British military to make soldiers more aggressive.

7

The Legal Context of
the Feminist Debate

As we suggested in Chapter 1, proponents of the different discourses on pornography compete with each other to persuade political audiences that their claims and prescriptions for social action are valid. Implicit in the various feminist perspectives are divergent views regarding the nature of the state and the law. The feminist movement has always been marked by disagreement over whether patriarchal legal systems can be effectively used to advance women's interests and whether special protective legislation for women will be used against women (Baron 1987). Currently, feminists concerned about the pornography issue have been forced to respond to traditional (nonfeminist) political-legal discourses and strategies that have excluded consideration of gender. Prior to the innovative civil rights antipornography ordinance introduced by Andrea Dworkin and Catharine Mac-Kinnon in 1983, these traditional approaches dominated the political scene. What is indeed significant about the civil rights approach has been the attention it has attracted in nonfeminist spheres of influence. At the same time, it is precisely the civil rights approach that has most polarized the feminist community.

In this chapter, we situate the civil rights approach in the context of U.S. Supreme Court decisions on obscenity—the controlling legal discourse that sets limits on constitutionally permissible action with respect to pornography. We then evaluate the arguments for and against the civil rights approach. Finally, we consider alternative legal approaches to the regulation or control of pornography.

THE U.S. SUPREME COURT, THE FIRST AMENDMENT, AND OBSCENITY

The First Amendment to the Constitution of the United States states that "Congress shall make no law respecting an establishment of religion, or prohibiting the free exercise thereof; or abridging the freedom of speech, or of the press; or the right of the people peacefully to assemble, and to petition the Government for a redress of grievances."[1] The relevant section, which sets the context for any legal resolution of the contemporary pornography debate, refers to that portion of the amendment that deals with freedom of speech and press. The First Amendment was enacted in 1791, but the right to free speech has been precarious and its meaning and enforcement have had a tumultuous history. In the legal battles of the early twentieth century, the Court had ruled that speech could be restricted if it advocated unlawful action, posed a "clear and present danger" to society, or lacked redeeming social value (see Downs 1989; Kairys 1982; Penrod & Linz 1984). In the 1942 case of *Chaplinsky v. New Hampshire* the Court held that, irrespective of any "clear and present danger," the First Amendment does not protect certain categories of expression such as libel, fighting words, lewd and offensive speech, and obscenity because they serve "no essential part of any exposition of ideas, and are of such slight social value as a step to truth that any benefit that may be derived from them is clearly outweighed by the social interest in order and morality" (p. 572).

It is important to note that it was "obscenity," not "pornography," that was the relevant legal category for First Amendment deliberations.[2] Although it was not until *Roth v. United States* (1957) that the Supreme Court explicitly addressed the constitutionality of obscenity law as such, its legal definition can be traced to the 1868 English case of *Regina v. Hicklin*, where the court defined obscenity as material that tended "to deprave and corrupt those whose minds are open to such immoral influences" (p. 371). Under *Hicklin* material could be prohibited solely because of its sexual content and not, as had previously been the case, because it attacked the government or sacred religious institutions.

The *Hicklin* decision, which reflected a conservative view of sexual morality, was the prevailing approach to obscenity in the United States for several decades. In the 1930s a more liberal approach emerged as a U.S. federal district court and court of appeals ruled that James Joyce's *Ulysses* was constitutionally protected in spite of the fact that it contained some obscenity. As the district court indicated, the legal standard for obscenity required that the author had "pornographic intent" or that the work as a whole stirred the average reader's "sex impulses" or led to "sexually impure or lustful thoughts" (cited in Downs 1989, p. 12). The "effect of isolated passages on a susceptible reader no longer sufficed to make a work obscene" (p. 12).

In *Roth v. United States* (1957), a case involving the mailing of sexually oriented materials, the Supreme Court finally addressed the First Amendment implications of obscenity law. In this decision, Justice William Brennan asserted that obscenity was not protected by the First Amendment because it was "utterly without redeeming social importance" (p. 484). However, he narrowed *Hicklin* by defining obscenity in terms of "whether to the average person, applying contemporary community standards, the dominant theme of the material as a whole appeals to the prurient interest" (p. 489).

Because it was fraught with ambiguities regarding the meaning of key terms, *Roth* was only the beginning of the Court's efforts to define obscenity. In *Manual Enterprises v. Day* (1962), for instance, *Roth* was narrowed somewhat by requiring that the appeal to "prurient interest" be "patently offensive." In *Jacobellis v. Ohio* (1964), which is famous for Justice Stewart's "I know it when I see it" definition of obscenity, *Roth*'s "utterly without redeeming social importance" was interpreted as protecting works that contained "even minimally valuable material" (Downs 1989, p. 15). In the 1966 case of *A Book Called "John Cleland's Memoirs of a Woman of Pleasure" ("Fanny Hill") v. Attorney General of Massachusetts*, the emerging standards were brought together in a three-part test: "(a) the dominant theme of the material taken as a whole appeals to the prurient interest in sex; (b) the material is patently offensive because it affronts contemporary community standards relating to the description or representation of sexual matters; and (c) the material is utterly without redeeming social value" (pp. 419–20). Essentially, *Memoirs* ruled that only "hard-core" pornography or "worthless trash" that went "well beyond the limits of candor could be designated obscene" (Downs 1989, p. 16). As a consequence of this decision obscenity prosecutions dwindled and pornography was allowed to proliferate.

In 1969 the Court came close to completely legalizing pornography by ruling in *Stanley v. Georgia* that individuals had the right to possess obscene materials in the privacy of their own homes: "The right to receive information and ideas, regardless of their social worth, is fundamental to our free society" (p. 564). But under the leadership of newly appointed Chief Justice Warren Burger, the Court stopped short of institutionalizing "the ultimate liberal position" (Downs 1989, p. 16). In *Miller v. California* (1973) Chief Justice Burger abandoned the "minimal value" approach and elevated the quality of social value required to grant material First Amendment protection. Justice Burger's new three-part definition defined obscenity in terms of whether "(a) . . . the average person, applying contemporary community standards, would find that the work, taken as a whole, appeals to the prurient interest . . . ; (b) . . . the work depicts or describes, in a patently offensive way, sexual conduct specifically defined by . . . state law; and (c) . . . the work, taken as a whole, lacks serious literary, artistic, political, or scientific value" (p. 24).

In the final analysis, however, *Miller* differed little from *Memoirs*, for only patently offensive "hard-core" pornography could be prohibited. As "plain examples," Burger offered "patently offensive representations or descriptions of ultimate sexual acts, normal or perverted," or "patently offensive representations or descriptions of masturbation, excretory functions, and lewd exhibition of the genitals" (p. 25). On the other hand, *Miller* did shift the determinant of "community standards" from a national to local basis, allowing local juries to decide such standards, provided they acted in accordance with the other elements of *Miller*.[3]

Although constructed by a conservative chief justice, *Miller* did not result in increased prosecutions of pornography (Leventhal 1977). Donald Downs (1989) identifies several reasons for this, including confusion over the meaning of key terms in *Miller*, low priority given by prosecutors operating with scarce resources, public tolerance of freedom of choice, lack of societal consensus regarding the harms of pornography, and effective representation by experienced pornography attorneys. Radical feminists, as well as conservatives, have been frustrated by this state of affairs, noting that under Supreme Court guidelines pornography (including violent pornography) has been allowed to proliferate (MacKinnon 1984, 1986). MacKinnon observes that the terms of *Miller* require jurors (finders of fact) to admit that they find material that sexually arouses them to be patently offensive. She also notes that the profitability of pornography itself has helped to construct community standards since the "more pornography exists in a community, the more likely it is that community standards will de facto come to correspond to it" (1986, p. 39). In addition, she asks, if a woman was violated in the making of a pornographic film, "Why should it matter that the work has other value?" (1984, p. 332).

Obscenity law treats pornography (or rather "obscenity") as a "term without specific implications for gender relations" (Elmer 1988, p. 51). According to MacKinnon (1984), obscenity law is concerned with questions of sexual morality and sin, of good and evil, from the male point of view. It is not so much aimed at protecting individuals from harm as at maintaining the "purity" of the community. From a radical feminist perspective, materials that are nonproblematic (for example, depictions of consensual homosexual activity) are criminalized, while materials that are harmful (for example, the eroticization of violence) are protected. By not exposing its gendered foundations, obscenity law "proceeds oblivious to—and serves to disguise the presence and interest of—the position of power that underlies . . . and is furthered by [it]" (p. 330). MacKinnon also questions the epistemological basis of Justice Stewart's "I know it when I see it" standard: "If I ask, from the point of view of women's experiences, does he know what I know when I see what I see, I find that I doubt it, given what's on the newsstands. How does his point of view keep what is there, there?" (p. 325).

THE CIVIL RIGHTS APPROACH

As we indicated earlier, feminist antipornography activists, led by Dworkin and MacKinnon, rallied behind a civil rights approach that was designed to empower women by giving them the option of civil suit against those whose involvement with pornography caused harm to women. In this section, we examine the arguments for and against the civil rights approach.

Arguments For the Civil Rights Approach

Radical feminists argue that it has not been possible to effectively prevent the harm associated with pornography under the hegemony of obscenity law. They have developed an alternative legal approach that utilizes the discourse of civil rights rather than the discourse of obscenity. The first civil rights antipornography ordinance was introduced in Minneapolis in 1983; similar versions later appeared in Indianapolis and other localities.[4] The ordinance was unique in its attempt to legally define pornography as sex discrimination and as a violation of women's civil rights. This approach is comparable to the treatment of sexual harassment, school segregation, and employment discrimination as civil rights violations (MacKinnon 1985). Although men, children, and transsexuals are covered by its provisions, the ordinance is based on the argument that pornography differentially harms women. It states that pornography hinders:

opportunities for equality . . . in employment, education, property rights, public accommodations and public services; create[s] public harassment and private denigration; promote[s] injury and degradation such as rape, battery and prostitution and inhibit[s] just enforcement of laws against these acts; contribute[s] . . . to restricting women from full exercise of citizenship and participation in public life . . . ; damage[s] relationships between the sexes; and undermine[s] women's equal exercise of rights to speech and action. (Dworkin & MacKinnon 1988, pp. 99–100)

The ordinance defines pornography as the graphic, "sexually explicit subordination of women," whether in pictures or words, that includes one of more of the following:

(i) women are presented dehumanized as sexual objects, things or commodities; or (ii) women are presented as sexual objects who enjoy pain or humiliation; or (iii) women are presented as sexual objects who experience sexual pleasure in being raped; or (iv) women are presented as sexual objects tied up or cut up or mutilated or bruised or physically hurt; or (v) women are presented in postures of sexual submission; or (vi) women's body parts . . . are exhibited, such that women are reduced to those parts; or (vii) women are presented as whores by nature; or (viii) women are presented being penetrated by objects or animals; or (ix) women are presented in scenarios of degradation, injury, [and so on] . . . in a context that makes these conditions sexual. (p. 101)

This civil rights approach is intended to empower women by giving them the choice to directly confront pornography and initiate civil suit against those who cause harm by trafficking in pornography, coercing people into pornographic performance, forcing pornography on people, or assaulting people in a way that is directly caused by specific pornography. According to its framers, the mere existence of pornographic materials does not make them actionable (Dworkin & MacKinnon 1988). Only alleged victims could initiate a lawsuit, and they "would have to *prove* that the challenged materials actually subordinated women in their making or use" (p. 39). The ordinance is not a criminal law that would either remove materials from circulation prior to a judicial determination or empower prosecutors to take independent action or request police seizure of materials (Dworkin 1985; MacKinnon 1984, 1985).

Liberals and civil libertarians, both feminist and nonfeminist, contend that the antipornography ordinance violates the First Amendment protection of free speech. They believe we must protect the speech of pornographers in order to protect everyone's speech. One of the liberal principles of free speech is that no particular viewpoint be officially sanctioned (Downs 1989). Insofar as liberals and civil libertarians remain unconvinced that pornography constitutes a harm to society, they argue that pro-ordinance advocates are attempting to impose a viewpoint-based regulation of speech which endorses a socially approved view of male-female relationships.

Pro-ordinance advocates argue that the First Amendment was designed primarily to protect political speech and dissent, and that "speech that lies at the periphery of constitutional concern may be regulated on the basis of a lesser showing of government interest than speech that lies at the 'core' " (Sunstein 1986a, p. 29). They hold that much that could be considered pornographic lies far from this core, since in purpose and effect, it promotes sexual arousal rather than community deliberation on public and private issues. They acknowledge that viewpoint-based regulations of speech pose particular First Amendment difficulties, but argue that the ordinance aims at concrete harms. In fact, pro-ordinance feminists believe that the harm recognized by the ordinance "meets a higher standard" than has been required for existing exceptions to the First Amendment (MacKinnon 1986, p. 47).

According to radical feminists, women's speech is now often "silenced" by the free speech of men (and pornographers) (Dworkin 1985). Pornography makes public space dangerous for women, and consequently, women cannot freely participate in society and public forums. They are also unrepresented or misrepresented in cultural products. Radical feminists argue that the civil rights ordinance is designed to promote women's free speech or, in other words, to give women's speech social meaning. Liberal theory assumes that individuals, not groups, have rights, and that the First Amendment treats the speech of groups neutrally (Downs 1989). But, MacKinnon (1984) argues, the First Amendment assertion that freedom of speech shall not be abridged implies that free speech does in fact exist for all and that subgroups of the population are not now "silenced socially" in a systematic way (p. 340). MacKinnon finds this assumption untenable because "in a society of gender inequality the speech of the powerful impresses its view upon the world, concealing the truth of powerlessness under that despairing acquiescence which provides the appearance of consent and makes protest inaudible as well as rare" (pp. 336–7). Thus, for radical feminism, which is both the dissenting and the silenced point of view, "the urgent issue of freedom of speech is not primarily the avoidance of state intervention as such, but finding an affirmative means to get access to speech for those to whom it has been denied" (p. 340). Essentially, radical feminists argue that "affirmative action" or "progressive censorship" (see Marcuse 1969) with respect to the First Amendment is necessary for women to achieve free speech equity with men. Just as affirmative action is viewed as necessary for advancing the employment and educational opportunities of women and minority groups, restricting the speech of pornographers is seen as necessary for achieving First Amendment rights for women. Under conditions of gender inequality, protecting pornographers' speech amounts to protecting sexual exploitation and males' right of sexual access to women (Barry 1979; Dworkin 1985).

Arguments Against the Civil Rights Approach

The Minneapolis ordinance was passed twice by the city council and vetoed twice by the mayor. A similar ordinance was later passed in Indianapolis, but was ruled unconstitutional (for reasons we will discuss below) in an opinion written by Federal District Court Judge Sarah Barker (*American Booksellers Association, Inc. v. Hudnut* 1984; Barker 1986). Judge Barker's ruling was affirmed in an opinion by Judge Frank Easterbrook (1984) of the Seventh Circuit Court of Appeals (Baldwin 1986; Easterbrook 1989), and affirmed without an opinion by the U.S. Supreme Court (1986). The Feminist Anti-Censorship Taskforce (FACT) was the key feminist organization that challenged the constitutionality of the ordinance. FACT's public opposition to the civil rights approach forced many feminists to take sides in spite of their reservations about both the FACT and the Dworkin-MacKinnon positions (Rich 1985).

For FACT, the free speech accorded to pornographers is necessary to guarantee free speech for feminists and to allow the creation of feminist erotica (Duggan et al. 1985; Hunter & Law 1985). While radical feminists argue that the civil rights approach to pornography does not involve censorship, FACT argues that its censoring impact or "chilling effect" would be as great as that of obscenity law. Similarly, Downs (1989) believes that although the ordinance does not involve criminal prosecution or prior restraint, "civil actions can be as censorial in their effects as criminal actions and . . . penalties or punishments after publication can inhibit expression as effectively as prior restraint" (p. 156; see *New York Times v. Sullivan* 1964).

Moreover, FACT argues that there is no guarantee that the ordinance would be implemented in a manner consistent with feminist goals and fears it could be used by nonfeminist conservatives to restrict materials they found objectionable (Duggan et al. 1985). FACT's concerns arose partly in response to the local politics surrounding the ordinance's passage in Indianapolis. Although radical feminists were at the forefront of efforts to pass the ordinance in Minneapolis,[5] conservatives led the way in Indianapolis (Downs 1989). The legislation was sponsored by a "conservative Republican stop-ERA activist" and supported by groups such as Citizens for Decency and the Coalition for a Clean Community (Duggan et al. 1985, p. 132). Although MacKinnon was brought in to draft the ordinance and serve as a consultant, she was kept "behind the scenes," for proponents "did not want to risk alienating the [conservative] council with her radical feminism" (Downs 1989, p. 113). Key council members viewed MacKinnon "as a conservative, and they did not know about her background" (p. 113). All feminists who made public statements opposed the legislation, which was "passed in a council meeting packed with 300 religious fundamentalists" (Duggan et al. 1985, p. 133). The twenty-four Republicans on the council voted in favor of passage, while the five Democrats voted against.

FACT also notes that although the state would not be authorized to initiate cases under the civil rights approach, judges (generally with a male view of pornography) would have the ultimate authority to award monetary damages or issue an injunction preventing further distribution of the materials in question (Duggan et al. 1985). Furthermore, FACT argues that no "direct harm" has to be proven since under the "trafficking" section of the ordinance "any woman" (or man or transsexual) "acting against the subordination of women . . . has a cause of action" (see Dworkin & MacKinnon 1988, p. 102). And, FACT adds, insofar as the ordinance defines pornography as harmful, a plaintiff only has to "convince the judge that the material corresponds to some term of the definition" (Waring 1986, p. 88). Other critics argue that under the "assault" section "material that simply depicted women in positions of 'humiliation' . . . [are] grounds for action if some vulnerable individual committed a sexual assault" following exposure, thus allowing the "reaction of the most degenerate reader or viewer . . . [to] determine what the remainder of the population" could read or see (Downs 1989, p. 158; Tigue 1985, p. 105).

FACT is particularly critical of the ordinance's definition of pornography, which prohibits not only "images of gross sexual violence that most supporters claim to be its target, but . . . drifts toward covering an increasingly wide range of sexually explicit materials" (Duggan et al. 1985, p. 135). Although a central component of the definition of pornography deals with materials that depict "sexually explicit subordination," the term "subordination" is never defined. According to FACT, the pro-ordinance brief in the Indianapolis case invokes its own version of Justice Stewart's standard by suggesting that the average person can decide what is pornographic on the basis of "his or her common understanding of what it means for one person to subordinate another" (p. 140). But Duggan et al. assert that

to some, any graphic sexual act violates women's dignity and therefore subordinates them. To others, consensual heterosexual lovemaking within the boundaries of procreation and marriage is acceptable, but heterosexual acts that do not have reproduction as their aim lower women's status and hence subordinate them. Still others accept a wide range of nonprocreative, perhaps, even nonmarital, heterosexuality but draw the line at lesbian sex, which they view as degrading. (p. 140)

Similar ambiguities of meaning are seen to exist with the ordinance's concern with women treated as "sex objects . . . or commodities," or as sex objects "tied up," or with women shown in "scenarios of degradation," or "as whores by nature," or in "postures of sexual submission." These clauses, according to Duggan et al., "have little to do with violence at all" and actually target material that is "sexually explicit and sexist" (p. 137).[6]

Expressing implicit agreement with many of FACT's arguments, but emphasizing the constitutional issues set forth in

Miller, Federal District Judge Barker in the Indianapolis case argued that the speech restricted by the ordinance was even broader than the speech restricted by *Miller* (Barker 1986). She was unconvinced of the need to create a new "class of constitutionally unprotected speech, labeled 'pornography' and characterized as sexually discriminatory" (p. 170), or of the need to provide women as a group with the same legal protection as children.[7] She did not agree that the ordinance was concerned with harm rather than the content of speech, and thus found it viewpoint-based. Seventh Circuit Judge Easterbrook concurred, arguing that the ordinance sought to control and influence attitudes and social relations "on a large scale," and that proponents had not demonstrated that injuries "inexorably follow" from pornography (cited in Baldwin 1986, pp. 81–82). Downs (1989) adds that the ordinance made "even isolated passages grounds for action, unlike obscenity law in which a work's dominant theme, taken as a whole, must be prurient, . . . [and that] a work could be held to be pornographic regardless of redeeming social value" (p. 155).[8]

Judge Barker implied that a civil rights ordinance in and of itself, if it met the standards of *Miller* and resolved problems of overbreadth, might be constitutional. Overbreadth, as Cass Sunstein (1986a) points out, refers to "the concern . . . that in the course of regulating unprotected speech, government may in the process censor speech that is not subject to control" (p. 35). Sunstein argues that overbreadth is always a problem in regulatory legislation but is never, in itself, a sufficient justification for "doing nothing about a significant problem." Regarding the ordinance, he suggests that the overbreadth problem might be resolved if legislation distinguished between visual media, especially films, and written work, and focused on work "considered as a whole" that lacked "serious literary, artistic, or other value" (p. 36). He also believes that "regulable pornography" should focus on "sexually explicit," violence-oriented material since the most compelling evidence indicates that this is the principal source of pornography's harm (1986b, p. 529.) Many radical feminists would reject this approach because it relies too heavily on the *Miller* standard and would substantially narrow the protections the ordinance was designed to provide. Other feminists, at this point, might be more willing to compromise, although concerns about definitional ambiguity would have to be addressed in order for a revised civil rights ordinance to achieve more widespread acceptance.[9]

ALTERNATIVE LEGAL APPROACHES

While radical feminists have made the civil rights ordinance the keystone of their antipornography campaign, Lauren Robel (1989) recommends taking a more serious look at other available remedies for the pornography problem. At the same time, she finds the civil rights approach valuable as a "theoretical construct" that helps focus attention on what might be accomplished through existing law (p. 190).

Trafficking in Pornography

In some sense, the heart of the ordinance is the trafficking section, which makes actionable the "production, sale, exhibition, or distribution of pornography" solely because of its discriminatory effects (Dworkin & MacKinnon 1988, p. 101). Robel (1989) suggests, however, that the problem with existing (constitutionally permissible) remedies for decreasing the availability of "hardcore" pornography is not that they cannot work, but that they are not systematically enforced. Although more rigorous enforcement of obscenity law "would not achieve a rethinking of the message of pornography," it could go a long way toward eliminating much pornography that feminists find objectionable (p. 189). Robel notes that in cities where obscenity law enforcement has been made a priority, such as in Atlanta and Cincinnati, this has been accomplished to a large extent. She adds that it will probably be easier to lobby to increase these efforts than to gain acceptance of a new legal theory. Similarly, Wendy Kaminer (1980) observes that it is easier to demonstrate that a particular work is obscene than it is to prove that it poses an "immediate danger" (p. 245). Moreover, feminists themselves can contribute to the public debate about "community standards" and hence lend direction to enforcement priorities.

Downs (1989) recommends a compromise strategy that might make obscenity law more consistent with feminist goals: accept the basic three-part framework of *Miller* but add a fourth prong that would deal with "violent obscenity." This approach would incorporate feminist concerns about violence into obscenity law and narrow *Miller* to material that receives the greatest public support for legal restriction:

Miller has been adjudicated since 1973 and reflects over thirty years of Supreme Court rulings. . . . Endorsing [it] . . . means affirming certain norms concerning sexual expressions as well as acknowledging the limits of efforts to censor. . . . Miller's logic can . . . embrace the values of equal respect and personalization of desire . . . [while its] tolerance of most forms of pornography guards against the unrealistic attempt to exclude all forms of inegalitarian and depersonalized sex. . . . And by limiting the restriction of violent sex to obscene contexts, the relation between significant sexual arousal and violence would be underscored. (pp. 194–6)

Assault Due to Pornography

The assault provision of the ordinance, which allows claims against the assailant as well as the producer and distributor for an attack or injury "directly caused by specific pornography" (Dworkin & MacKinnon 1988, p. 103), potentially might be handled through existing criminal and civil remedies. For instance, since the mid-1970s most states have passed some form of rape reform legislation designed to eliminate the misogynist assumptions and prejudicial practices associated with the traditional criminal justice treatment of rape. But officials have been lax in their implementation of these reforms, and some reformed laws have retained problematic provisions (for example, exemptions that provide spouses and other intimates with immunity from prosecution) (Berger et al. 1988). Robel (1989) suggests that feminists focus on improving the nature and enforcement of this body of criminal law, as well as existing tort (civil) law that allows victims to be compensated by assailants for personal injury or harm. Current remedies for female victims are inadequate not because of existing law as such, but because of "the persistent failure of those who enforce the law to recognize and credit injury in sexual contexts," especially when perpetuated by individuals previously known to the victim (p. 181).

On the other hand, holding the producers and distributors of pornography accountable for the actions of third-party assailants is much more difficult. While existing product liability law allows civil action against a manufacturer or distributor of a commercial product for wrongful or negligent conduct, the plaintiff (victim) in a pornography case would have to demonstrate that the assault committed by the third-party (assailant) would not have occurred but for the defendant's (manufacturer/distributor) misconduct. In other words, to recover damages against the producer or distributor of pornography, it would have to be shown that the assailant's exposure to specific pornographic materials was a "necessary precondition" or "dominant cause" of the plaintiff's injury (Linz et al. 1984, pp. 279, 281). A causal connection would have to be made between a particular depiction of harm-producing behavior and a particular harm-producing behavior. It would not be sufficient to assert that such materials were "widely available" or that they promoted aggressive tendencies in general. It would likely be necessary to show, for instance, that a plaintiff's "injury resembled in some unique detail a similar rape enacted in materials viewed by the rapist," that the "rapist learned his particular method from the film depiction" (an instructional effect), and that the "rapist was motivated by the depiction to reenact what he had learned" (an incitement effect) (Donnerstein et al. 1987, pp. 156–7; see Hilker 1979). All this would be extremely difficult to demonstrate, especially in light of social science research which indicates that some types of individuals are more predisposed than others to the negative influences of pornography (see Chapter 6).

Thus there are substantial problems involved in translating existing product liability law into the arena of pornography, and no court has yet accepted the notion that the contents of films, books, or magazines are the types of "products" that are covered by the law (Robel 1989). Under existing Supreme Court guidelines established in *Brandenburg v. Ohio* (1969), the specific pornography in question would have to "incite" rather than merely "advocate" lawless action, and the harm from the material would need to be not merely possible but "imminent." Following the logic of product liability law, one would also have to show that the defendant had not attempted to limit distribution of the pornography to individuals most likely to misuse the product (for example, minors too immature to evaluate its potentially harmful effects), that warnings about the product's potential harms were not made available to users (or, in the case of children, to parents), and that the product had a defective design (that is, a harmful message) that could have been removed but was not (Linz et al. 1984).

Nevertheless, Linz et al. (1984) believe that social science research is beginning to convincingly demonstrate that there are certain "risky" materials, that is, *"portrayals of rapes or other forms of sexual assault that show the female victim becoming involuntarily aroused or otherwise responding positively to sexual aggression"* (p. 292). Since the Supreme Court has to some extent allowed the marketplace (that is, community standards) to regulate pornography, "it may be appropriate to ascribe the same limitations to obscene materials as to any other potentially dangerous product" (p. 283). Thus producers and distributors of pornography might be required not only to limit access to minors and provide warnings, but also to offer some sort of debriefing or epilogue that corrects the harmful message ("design defect") of the material. Linz et al. argue that such corrective devices could be incorporated into most material at little cost to producers and that failure to do so might establish a case of negligence.

Forcing Pornography on a Person

The ordinance is also concerned with situations where an individual is involuntarily exposed to pornography. In the public arena there are a number of existing remedies that might be used more effectively to achieve this objective. For instance, sexual harassment laws could be logically expanded to cover exposure to pornography in the workplace. In *Meritor Savings Bank, FSB v. Vinson* (1986), the Supreme Court held that Title VII of the Civil Rights Act of 1964, which prohibits sex discrimination in employment, also covers sexual harassment that creates a "hostile" workplace, provided the harassment was "sufficiently severe or pervasive to alter the conditions of . . . employment and create an abusive working environment" (cited in Robel 1989, p. 184; see MacKinnon 1979).

In addition, regulations concerning the manner in which sexually explicit materials may be displayed for sale in stores (for example, placing material behind the counter or in segregated "adults only" sections, packaging material in plastic or opaque covers) might be employed and found constitutionally acceptable, especially if such laws were designed to prevent exposure to minors (see *Ginsberg v. New York* 1968) or were "prompted by concern about the *effects* of the material" and not merely a desire to suppress their content (Robel 1989, p. 185). Some have also suggested increased use of zoning laws that regulate businesses specializing in sexually oriented materials, as zoning laws have been viewed favorably by the Court (*Young v. American Mini Theatres* 1976; *Renton v. Playtime Theatres, Inc.* 1986). However, these laws are problematic because pornographic businesses tend to be relegated to predominantly poor and minority communities, unfairly impacting on certain segments of society (White 1985).

Fewer remedies exist for regulating involuntary exposure to pornography in the home. Robel (1989) notes that existing tort remedies for "intentional or negligent infliction of emotional distress" might be applied—for instance, in the case of a woman who had been tied down by her husband and forced to watch pornographic films (p. 184).

Coercion into Pornographic Performance

The provision of the ordinance concerned with coercing, intimidating, or fraudulently inducing a person into performing for pornography might be handled through existing laws dealing with contracts made under conditions of fraud or duress (Duggan et al. 1985). In cases where photographs or films are taken surreptitiously, are taken under conditions of abuse or intimidation (as was the case with Linda Marchiano), or are taken voluntarily but put on public display without one's consent, existing tort law recognizes several ways a case might be actionable for invasion of privacy, libel, or defamation of character. For instance, a case might be actionable when the involuntary use of the pornography results in someone receiving unreasonable publicity, being placed in a false light, being represented in a way that distorts the truth, or suffering significant harm to his or her reputation (Osanka & Johann 1989; Robel 1989).[10] In a federal court case, for example, a woman who had consented to having her nude photos published in *Playboy* successfully sued when the photos were sold without her consent (a consent form was forged) to *Hustler* (*Douglass v. Hustler Magazine, Inc.* 1986). The court agreed with the plaintiff that "being depicted in voluntary association with a magazine with the editorial viewpoint of *Hustler*" placed her in a "false light" insofar as the magazine was known for its "hostility to or contempt for racial, ethnic, and religious minorities" (cited in Robel 1989, pp. 187, 194).[11]

CONCLUSION

Because they were dissatisfied with traditional obscenity law, antipornography feminists were attracted to the promise of a new and innovative civil rights approach to pornography. Although proponents continue to hope that modified civil rights ordinances will eventually satisfy constitutional scrutiny (Dworkin & Mac-Kinnon 1988; Osanka & Johann 1989), some feminists have called for a renewed focus on remedies that are available in existing law. MacKinnon (1986), however, finds this latter view too limited. She believes that relying on existing law amounts to displaying "a peculiar complacency in the face of human suffering, since the legal status quo has rather obviously permitted the suffering which constitutes the social status quo" (p. 47). On the other hand, Wendy Kaminer (1990) argues that any erosion of First Amendment rights will be detrimental to feminists' ability to express their point of view. She notes that while pro-ordinance advocates proclaim that "pornography silences women," it did not silence them, and it "is more than a little crazy for women to think that censorship will make them free" (p. 202–3). Nevertheless, Gordon Hawkins and Franklin Zimring (1988) observe that resolution of the contemporary debate should not require acceptance of the "false antithesis . . . that there are only two possible collective responses to pornography as a social issue: the imposition of censorship or the toleration of anarchy" (p. 198). What will most likely be required will be a "willingness to compromise and the need to balance competing legitimate claims" (Downs 1989, p. xix).

NOTES

1. Parts of this and the following section were originally developed in Ronald Berger, Patricia Searles, and Charles Cottle (1990a).

2. The term "obscenity" is of Latin derivation, meaning "filth" or that which "takes place offstage," and came to refer to that which was repulsive, offensive, or disgusting. The term "pornography" is of Greek derivation, meaning the "writing of harlots" or depictions of acts of prostitutes, and came to refer to that which was sexually explicit. Traditionally, obscenity and pornography were not synonymous, and pornography was not viewed as obscene. However, the U.S. Supreme Court has blurred the distinction between the two (Penrod & Linz 1984).

3. In *Jenkins v. Georgia* (1974) the Court ruled that "nudity" alone could not be held obscene. In *Pope v. Illinois* (1987) the Court ruled that juries must determine lack of serious value according to the standards of a "reasonable person" not merely prevailing community standards.

4. Ordinances have also been proposed in Bellingham, Washington; Cambridge, Massachusetts; Los Angeles, California; Madison, Wisconsin; and Suffolk County, New York (Osanka & Johann 1989).

5. On the basis of evidence derived from the official transcripts of the hearings and interviews with key participants, Downs (1989) is critical of the way pro-ordinance forces in Minneapolis staged the testimony (during council hearings) in favor of passage, used emotionally charged rhetoric and hyperbole, stifled dissenting views, lacked respect for "competing legitimate values," and "railroaded the ordinance through" without consulting the appropriate city offices (pp. 65–66). However, he is also critical of the Minnesota Civil Liberties Union which "would agree to no restrictions on [pornography] whatsoever, . . . made light of concerns about the more violent material," and demonstrated an "intransigent, knee-jerk opposition [that] compounded the problem" (pp. 65, 91).

6. In the Indianapolis ordinance, according to Dworkin and Mac-Kinnon (1988), "violence *must* be shown *in the material itself* for a trafficking claim to be made," but if violence occurs in the making or use of the material, a victim of coercion or assault may sue even if the material itself does not show violence" (p. 40).

7. In *New York v. Ferber* (1982) the Court ruled that it was permissible to prohibit the sale and distribution of child pornography in order to prevent harm to children. The court reasoned that this would be more effective than prohibiting the use of children without directly attacking the "speech" (Sunstein 1986a).

8. Although the Indianapolis ordinance "modified the first problem in its revision of the [Minneapolis] ordinance, . . . the second problem remained" (Downs 1989, p. 155).

9. Recently, Frank Osanka & Sara Johann (1989) drew upon existing civil rights, obscenity, and child pornography law to develop an "Anti-Sexual Exploitation Act" that contains both civil and criminal remedies and that may be used in "conjunction with current laws" (p. 422). This "model pornography law," as they describe it, focuses on "violent and degrading" pornography and on child pornography. It attempts to improve the language of earlier civil rights ordinances by

more clearly specifying the types of pornographic representations and actionable behaviors that are covered. Although Osanka and Johann recognize that parts of their proposed law, like the Indianapolis ordinance, raise constitutional questions, they offer it as a way to move beyond the legal status quo.

10. Libel laws afford less protection to public figures because the Supreme Court has required that such plaintiffs establish a "higher level of fault . . . to recover damages" (Robel 1989, p. 188; see *New York Times v. Sullivan* 1964). Some feminists advocate a group libel approach, especially where the pornography in question is racist—for example, when black women are depicted as animals (Bart 1985; Tong 1984). However, the courts have been unsympathetic to group libel approaches since 1978, when the federal courts upheld the right of Nazis to march in Skokie, Illinois, a community where a number of Holocaust survivors reside (Downs 1985, 1989).

11. *Hustler* has been the defendant in several cases of this sort (see Robel 1989).

8

Nonlegal Alternatives and Concluding Remarks

Religious-conservatives support governmental regulations of private behavior that enforce traditional values. Antipornography feminists, in contrast, are concerned about the government using its power to buttress the status quo, although they have been willing to use the legal system to help achieve their objectives (Cottle et al. 1989). In the first major collection of articles published by antipornography feminists, Wendy Kaminer (1980) cautioned feminists not to look to the state to eliminate pornography.

The feminist movement against pornography must remain an anti-defamation movement, involved in education, consciousness-raising, and the development of private strategies against the industry. . . . We can and should speak out, and take action against pornographers because they comprise a hostile group with interests antithetical to our own, . . . but we cannot ask the government to speak for us. . . . Legislative and judicial control is simply not possible without breaking down the legal principles and procedures that are essential to our own right to speak and, ultimately, our freedom to control our lives. (p. 247)

Rosemarie Tong (1984) made a similar point about feminists' reliance on law to achieve their objectives for social change.

> In a pluralistic society where moral and cultural diversity is not only tolerated but celebrated, and where institutions such as religion, education, and the family are relatively weak, increasing emphasis is placed on the law both as a means of social control and as a vehicle for social transformation. . . . But [the law is] . . . not always the only or the best answer to women's social problems, especially when these problems have sexual dimensions. . . . Women must realize that at best the law can curb sexual violence against women. . . . If feminists wish to create and maintain a sexual morality that liberates women, men, and children of all races, classes, and sexual preferences, they will have to transform not only the law, but education, religion, and the family. (pp. 3–4, 206)

In light of these observations, we encourage a careful investigation of nonlegal strategies vis-à-vis pornography. Further development and implementation of such strategies might encourage recognition of greater common ground between antipornography feminists and those anticensorship feminists who acknowledge the problems associated with much contemporary pornography (see Kaminer 1980, 1990; Rich 1980, 1985).

NONLEGAL STRATEGIES

Neil Malamuth (1985) identifies two *political-economic* and two *educational* approaches for dealing with pornography. The political-economic approaches include cooperative consultation and pressure confrontation, while the educational approaches include indirect and direct interventions. The cooperative consultation approach involves citizen/consumer groups monitoring available media and attempting to negotiate with producers and distributors of pornography (by writing letters, meeting with industry executives, and working with producers and writers) to revise the content of their media products. The pressure confrontation approach entails groups organizing boycotts, staging demonstrations and other protests, and engaging in various forms of civil disobedience that target the pornography industry in general or particular pornography enterprises or products. Indirect educational strategies involve interventions that address broad areas of behavior such as general sex education and critical media-viewing skills. Direct educational strategies entail interventions that deal specifically with pornography or the cultural myths and attitudes that contribute to violence against women.

Political-Economic Approaches

The cooperative approach has been fairly successful in persuading commercial media to develop programming that deals more constructively with social problems such as alcohol and drug abuse (see Breed & De Foe 1982). Similarly, feminist and pro-feminist groups have encouraged mainstream media to present women and men in less traditional and more egalitarian gender roles and to remove sexist imagery in advertising (Leidholdt 1983). To be sure, not all media organizations will be receptive to such collaboration, unless they perceive that eliminating particular content will advance their interests. For instance, there is some indication that *Playboy* publisher Hugh Hefner did respond to public concerns and research evidence regarding aggressive/violent pornography by cautioning his editors about using violent imagery in *Playboy* (Donnerstein et al. 1987). It is also possible that the publishers and producers of "soft-core" pornography may be more sensitive to objections regarding pornographic violence because of concerns about losing advertisers and distributing outlets (for example, general merchandise stores). They may even understand that acquiring a reputation which associates them with such content could deny them the social legitimacy they may seek. As Gordon Hawkins and Franklin Zimring (1988) note: "Hugh Hefner wants to be remembered as a philosopher, not as a sexist or an advocate of sexual violence" (p. 206).

Additional industry self-regulation through refinement of the existing film rating system would also be consistent with the cooperative approach. Currently, the film industry has institutionalized a voluntary rating scheme, administered by the Motion Picture Association of America, that identifies G, PG, PG-13, R, NC-17, and X ratings. A problem with these categories is that they do not provide sufficient information to viewers (and parents) regarding the criteria for the rating: Does the rating refer to language, violence, simple nudity, adult situations, sexual explicitness, or some combination of these? For instance, Edward Donnerstein, Daniel Linz, and Steven Penrod (1987) "find it curious that under the present system, the whole genre of slasher films, which graphically depict mutilation of women and which may be desensitizing viewers, fall into the same rating category as films that contain no sex or violence but that have two or more instances of the 'harsher sexually derived words' " (p. 168). The current voluntary approach could be fine-tuned to better inform viewers and to clearly identify "particular types of combination of sex and violence or . . . the outrageous degradation of women" (Hawkins & Zimring 1988, p. 207). Film producers' incorporation of educational pre-film briefings or post-film debriefings regarding the messages conveyed in the material might also become part of the revised advisory/rating scheme (see Chapter 6).

On the other hand, many feminists undoubtedly would find the cooperative approach ("negotiating with the enemy") problematic since it might seem to imply approval of or license for particular enterprises. Some would prefer more confrontational strategies in addition to or instead of cooperative ones. For instance, antipornography feminists' protest of the "I'm black and blue from the Rolling Stones" billboard (which included defacing the billboard; see Chapter 3) succeeded in getting Warner Brothers to remove the advertisement. Other strategies suggested by antipornography feminists include: (1) organizing protests in front of pornography shops and confronting customers; (2) organizing protests and boycotts of general merchandise stores that sell pornography; (3) organizing boycotts of nonpornographic products of corporations that also produce or distribute pornography; and (4) exposing magazines, newspapers, companies, and political officials who profit from pornography by publicly naming their sources of financial backing (Morgan 1978).

Educational Approaches

Indirect educational interventions, such as general sex education, that make people more knowledgeable about sexuality and interpersonal relationships would presumably make individuals less vulnerable to the influence of misogynist cultural media. These programs could teach individuals about traditional gender roles and alternatives, male and female sexuality and sexual scripts, and male and female differences in interpreting interaction "signals," and they could encourage more effective communication skills and egalitarian communication styles (Malamuth 1985; see Abbey 1982).

Direct educational interventions could teach people to recognize and critically respond to rape myths prevalent in the culture in general and in the media in particular. Pornography's relationship to the problem of sexual violence could be explored; this could include an evaluation of the relevant social science evidence. Previous research indicates that such interventions can be effective in mitigating the adverse effects of exposure to aggressive/violent pornography and in reducing belief in rape myths (see Chapter 6). In addition, education about rape prevention and personal protection strategies would also be valuable (Scarles & Berger 1987).

Educational interventions that target particular types of individuals as well as mass audiences could be further developed. For instance, parents and teachers need specially designed materials to help them discuss these issues with young children. Particular attention also needs to be directed toward male (and female) adolescents who are beginning to explore their sexuality and to date, and who may be especially inclined to look to the media for information about "appropriate" sexual conduct (Donnerstein et al. 1987). Furthermore, educational strategies need to be sensitive to and attempt to counteract the fact that individuals may become aroused by sexual violence, even if shown these materials in an educational context. Unless countered, the sexual arousal experienced by some individuals may interfere with the attempted attitude change and instead reinforce existing beliefs (Malamuth 1985; see Lord et al. 1979). Similarly, the social context of pornographic consumption needs to be addressed and potential negative effects need to be countered in educational efforts. For instance, the reader will recall that male bonding occurs through the group consumption of pornography (see Chapter 5), and that research suggests that when males and females view sexually violent materials together, traditional gender roles are reinforced (Zillman et al. 1986; see Chapter 6). Finally, public service messages that help pornography addicts, other sexual addicts, and potential sexual abusers identify themselves and that suggest means of getting help would be a valuable intervention.[1]

CONCLUDING REMARKS

The nonlegal strategies discussed above are neither new nor ground-shaking. But because "the basic contours of public policy toward pornography have been set and are not likely to change soon," it seems especially important to pursue them (Hawkins & Zimring 1988, p. xii). Obscenity law, as interpreted by the U.S. Supreme Court, will likely remain the dominant framework within which pornography as a legal issue will be adjudicated. Feminists may continue to refine the civil rights approach in order to provide protection to those vulnerable to sexual harm (Dworkin & MacKinnon 1988; Osanka & Johann 1989), but unless new ordinances conform to the requirements of *Miller*, they will not likely survive challenge on constitutional grounds.[2] Whether or not efforts to revise the civil rights approach are successful, antipornography feminists have made substantial contributions in defining pornography as an important social issue demanding attention from the academic community, public officials, and the general public. The furor over the ordinance has forced traditional civil libertarians to take feminist concerns about pornography seriously. Civil libertarians can no longer reduce the antiporno-graphy movement to religious fundamentalism or mere sexual prudery. Moreover, the controversy has stimulated feminists on both sides of the issue to develop critiques of the traditional political-legal discourses on pornography that have failed to consider the significance of gender, and to develop new insights into the nature of sexuality and its representation. Nonfeminist scholars as well have made contributions to understanding the sociological and legal implications of pornography that they might not have otherwise made were it not for the controversy provoked by the feminist antipornography movement.

Nevertheless, it will be difficult for feminists to keep the issue of pornography a priority for public deliberation. Social problems compete with one another for public attention and for "a spot on the evening news" (Hilgartner & Bosk 1988, p. 73). For example, the public's concern about drugs and AIDS, and the debates over government interventions in these areas, have clearly achieved prominence over pornography; and feminists have renewed their focus on abortion rights and have made child care and maternity benefits priority issues (Kaminer 1990). Hawkins and Zimring (1988) sardonically note that the "half-life of pornography as a major public issue after the Meese Commission . . . was about one month" (p. 225). Post–Meese Commission news regarding pornography has been dominated by concerns about federal funding of the arts, homoerotic art (for example, the Robert Mapplethorpe exhibit in Cincinnati), and obscene music lyrics (for example, 2 Live Crew's album, *As Nasty as They Wanna Be*) (Mathews 1990). Public deliberations on these issues have been rather far removed from feminist analyses of pornography.[3]

We agree with Hawkins and Zimring (1988) that sexually explicit materials are likely to remain widely available. At the same time, those interested in the pornography issue are likely to continue their attempts to delegitimate at least the degrading and violent forms of pornography and to develop and implement nonlegal strategies that might mitigate their adverse effects. Men, as well as women, have broken their silence on pornography and will persist in confronting this issue. Social scientists will continue to research this issue and help refine our understanding of the effects of pornography, and both feminists and nonfeminists will continue to develop theoretical analyses of pornography.

The long-term impact on antipornography feminism of the federal courts' refusal to add pornography to the list of exceptions to the First Amendment is not yet clear. But if an analogy with class/labor issues is appropriate, it is no more likely that the courts would allow women control over this cornerstone of patriarchal ideology than they have allowed workers collective bargaining rights over the central operations of business enterprises (for example, capital investment) (see *Fibreboard Paper Products Corp. v. NLRB* 1964).

Nevertheless, ideologies are capable of persisting "in the face of facts that should raise questions" about their practical efficacy, if not their theoretical adequacy (Skidmore 1989, p. 320). Ideologies are, of course, useful and necessary; they allow individuals to make sense of their world and to engage in social action. Indeed, feminist ideologies have generated new and creative ways of thinking as well as innovative social change strategies. But ideologies can also be constraining, insulating adherents from constructive criticism and revised ways of thinking and inhibiting the coalition-building necessary to create a mass constituency capable of redressing social problems. Faced with opposition from both within and outside of the feminist movement, antipornography feminists may end up turning inward—speaking to the already converted and risking the alienation of many heterosexual women by suggesting they cannot achieve control over their own sexuality—rather than making the modifications necessary to attract the support of a broader audience.

Some feminists have called for forums that would move the feminist debate over pornography and sexuality beyond the "divisive name-calling" (Philipson 1984, p. 113). If feminists remain divided, however, the chance of successfully competing with and supplanting the nonfeminist discourses on pornography will be seriously impaired. When differing views of social reality conflict, political power becomes the final arbiter of disputes. Those social forces able to enlist the support of the state will have their point of view established through the rule of law.

NOTES

1. Further development of educational materials for couples seeking to improve their sex lives, but not wishing to become dependent upon pornographic materials for arousal, would also be useful.

2. Even the Meese Commission rejected the feminist critique of obscenity law when it endorsed the federal court's decision in the Indianapolis case (Vance 1986).

3. Ironically, conservative columnist George Will (1990) has been one of the few writers to analyze recent controversies over pornographic expression in terms that mirror feminist concerns about violence against women.

References

Abbey, Antonio. 1982. "Sex differences in attributions for friendly behavior: Do males misperceive females' friendliness?" *Journal of Personality and Social Psychology* 42:830–8.

Althusser, Louis. 1971. *Lenin and Philosophy and Other Essays*, trans. B. Brewster. New York: Monthly Review Press.

American Booksellers Association, Inc. v. Hudnut, 598 F. Supp. 1316 (1984); 771 F.2d 323 (1985); 106 S.Ct. 1664 (1986).

Ashley, Barbara Renchkovsky and David Ashley. 1984. "Sex as violence: The body against intimacy." *International Journal of Women's Studies* 7:352–71.

Attorney General's Commission on Pornography. 1986. Washington, D.C.: U.S. Department of Justice.

Bader, Eleanor J. 1987. "Anti-porn or anti-sex?" *Guardian* (April 22): 2.

Baldwin, Gordon B. 1986. "Pornography: The supreme court rejects call for new restrictions." *Wisconsin Women's Law Journal* 2:75–83.

Barbach, Lonnie. 1976. *For Yourself*. New York: Anchor Press.

Barker, Judge Sarah Evans. 1986. "Pornography and first amendment rights." Pp. 166–76 in M. E. Katsh (ed.), *Taking Sides: Clashing Views on Controversial Legal Issues*, second edition. Guilford, CT: Dushkin.

Baron, Ava. 1987. "Feminist legal strategies: The powers of difference." Pp. 474–503 in B. Hess and M. Ferree (eds.), *Analyzing Gender: A Handbook of Social Science Research.* Newbury Park, CA: Sage.

Baron, Larry and Murray A. Straus. 1987. "Four theories of rape: A macrosociological analysis." *Social Problems* 34:467–89.

———. 1989. *Four Theories of Rape in American Society: A State-Level Analysis.* New Haven, CT: Yale University Press.

Baron, Robert. 1979. "Heightened sexual arousal and physical aggression: An extension to females." *Journal of Research in Personality* 13:91–102.

Barry, Kathleen. 1979. *Female Sexual Slavery.* New York: New York University Press.

———. 1988. "Female sexual slavery: The problem, policies and cause of feminist action." Pp. 282–96 in E. Boneparth and E. Stoper (eds.), *Women, Power, and Policy: Toward the Year 2000.* New York: Pergamon Press.

Bart, Pauline B. 1985. "Pornography: Institutionalizing woman-hating and eroticizing dominance and submission for fun and profit." *Justice Quarterly* 2:283–92.

———. 1986. "Pornography: Hating women and institutionalizing dominance and submission for fun and profit: Response to Alexis M. Durham III." *Justice Quarterly* 3:103–5.

———. 1989. "Book Review" of C. MacKinnon's *Feminism Unmodified: Discourses on Life and Law. American Journal of Sociology* 95:538–9.

Bart, Pauline B., Linda Freeman, and Peter Kimball. 1985. "The different worlds of women and men: Attitudes toward pornography and responses to *Not a Love Story*—a film about pornography." *Women's Studies International Forum* 8:307–22.

Bart, Pauline B. and Margaret Jozsa. 1980. "Dirty books, dirty films, and dirty data." Pp. 204–17 in L. Lederer (ed.), *Take Back the Night.* New York: Morrow.

Bart, Pauline B. and Patricia O'Brien. 1985. *Stopping Rape: Successful Survival Strategies.* New York: Pergamon.

Bartky, Sandra L. 1982. "Narcissism, femininity, and alienation." *Social Theory and Practice* 8:127–43.

Baudrillard, Jean. 1981. *For a Critique of the Political Economy of the Sign,* trans. Charles Levin. St. Louis: Telos Press.

Beneke, Timothy. 1990. "Intrusive images and subjectified bodies: Notes on visual heterosexual porn." Pp. 168–87 in M. Kimmel 145(ed.), *Men Confront Pornography*. New York: Crown Books.

Benson, Donna Jean and Gregg E. Thompson. 1982. "Sexual harassment on a university campus: The confluence of authority relations, sexual interest and gender stratification." *Social Problems* 29:237–51.

Berger, John. 1977. *Ways of Seeing*. New York: Penguin.

Berger, Ronald J., Patricia Searles, and Charles E. Cottle. 1990a. "A camp divided: Feminists on pornography." Pp. 67–102 in G. Miller and J. Holstein (eds.), *Perspectives on Social Problems*, Volume 2. Greenwich, CT: JAI Press.

———. 1990b. "Ideological contours of the contemporary pornography debate: Divisions and alliances." *Frontiers: A Journal of Women Studies* 11:30–38.

Berger, Ronald J., Patricia Searles, and W. Lawrence Neuman. 1988. "The dimensions of rape reform legislation." *Law and Society Review* 22:329–57.

Berger, Ronald J., Patricia Searles, Richard G. Salem, and Beth Ann Pierce. 1986. "Sexual assault in a college community." *Sociological Focus* 19:1–26.

Berlin, Isaiah. 1969. *Four Essays on Liberty*. London: Oxford University Press.

Best, Joel. 1987. "Rhetoric in claims-making: Constructing the missing children problem." *Social Problems* 34:101–21.

Betzold, Michael. 1977. "How pornography shackles men and oppresses women." Pp. 45–8 in J. Snodgrass (ed.), *For Men Against Sexism*. Albion, CA: Times Change Press.

Boneparth, Ellen and Emily Stoper (eds.). 1988. *Women, Power, and Policy: Toward the Year 2000*, second edition. New York: Pergamon Press.

A Book Called "John Cleland's Memoirs of a Woman of Pleasure" v. Attorney General of Massachusetts, 383 U.S. 413 (1966).

Bowers v. Hardwick, 478 U.S. 186 (1986).

Brandenburg v. Ohio, 395 U.S. 444 (1969).

Breed, Warren and James R. De Foe. 1982. "Effecting media change: The role of cooperative consultation on alcohol topics." *Journal of Communication* 32:88–99.

Brod, Harry (ed.). 1987. *The Making of Masculinities: The New Men's Studies*. Boston: Allen and Unwin.

———. 1990. "Eros thanatized: Pornography and male sexuality." Pp. 190–206 in M. Kimmel (ed.), *Men Confront Pornography*. New York: Crown Books.

Bross, M. S. 1984. *Effect of Pre-film Messages on Viewer Perceptions of Slasher Films*. Master's thesis, University of Wisconsin-Madison.

Burgess, Ann Wolbert and Marieanne Lindequist. 1984. *Child Pornography and Sex Rings*. Lexington, MA: Lexington Books.

Burstyn, Varda. 1985a. "Political precedents and moral crusades: Women, sex, and the state." Pp. 4–31 in V. Burstyn (ed.), *Women Against Censorship*. Vancouver: Douglas and McIntyre.

———. 1985b. "Beyond despair: Positive strategies." Pp. 152–80 in V. Burstyn (ed.), *Women Against Censorship*. Vancouver: Douglas and McIntyre.

Burt, Martha R. 1980. "Cultural myths and supports for rape." *Journal of Personality and Social Psychology* 38:217–30.

Burton, Doris-Jean. 1989. "Public opinion and pornography policy." Pp. 133–46 in S. Gubar and J. Hoff (eds.), *For Adult Users Only: The Dilemma of Violent Pornography*. Bloomington: Indiana University Press.

Campbell, Douglas. 1990. "One man's pleasures: A response to Weiss." Pp. 99–101 in M. Kimmel (ed.), *Men Confront Pornography*. New York: Crown Books.

Chafe, William Henry. 1977. *Women and Equality: Changing Patterns in American Culture*. New York: Oxford University Press.

Chafetz, Janet Saltzman and Anthony Gary Dworkin. 1987. "In the face of threat: Organized antifeminism in comparative perspective." *Gender and Society* 1:33–60.

Champion, Cheryl A. 1986. "Clinical perspectives on the relationship between pornography and sexual violence." *Law and Inequality* 4:22–7.

Chancer, Lynn S. 1987. "New Bedford, Massachusetts, March 6, 1983–March 22, 1984: The 'before and after' of a group rape." *Gender and Society* 1:239–60.

Changing Men: Issues in Gender, Sex and Politics 15. 1985. Special issue on "Men Confronting Pornography."

Chaplinksy v. New Hampshire, 315 U.S. 568 (1942).

Chesney-Lind, Meda. 1989. "Girl's crime and woman's place: Toward a feminist model of female delinquency." *Crime and Delinquency* 35:5–29.

Chodorow, Nancy. 1990. *Feminism and Psychoanalytic Theory*. New Haven: Yale University Press.

Chow, Esther Ngan-Ling. 1987. "The development of feminist consciousness among Asian American women." *Gender and Society* 1:284–99.

Clark, Chris. 1985. "Pornography without power?" *Changing Men* 15:15–16.

Clark, Lorenne M. G. 1983. "Liberalism and pornography." Pp. 45–59 in D. Copp and S. Wendell (eds.), *Pornography and Censorship*. Buffalo: Prometheus.

Clark, Lorenne M. G. and Debra J. Lewis. 1977. *Rape: The Price of Coercive Sexuality*. Toronto: Canadian Women's Educational Press.

Cohen, Cheryl H. 1986. "The feminist sexuality debate: Ethics and politics." *Hypatia* 1:71–86.

Cole, Susan E. 1989. *Pornography and the Sex Crisis*. Toronto: Amantia.

Collins, Patricia Hill. 1986. "Learning from the outsider within: The sociological significance of black feminist thought." *Social Problems* 33:S14–S32.

Commission on Obscenity and Pornography. 1970. *The Report of the Commission on Obscenity and Pornography*. New York: Bantam Books.

Converse, Phillip E. 1964. "The nature of belief systems and mass publics." Pp. 206–61 in D. Apter (ed.), *Ideology and Discontent*. New York: Free Press.

Cottle, Charles E., Patricia Searles, Ronald J. Berger, and Beth Ann Pierce. 1989. "Conflicting ideologies and the politics of pornography." *Gender and Society* 3:303–33.

Court, John H. 1976. "Pornography and sex crimes: A re-evaluation in the light of recent trends throughout the world." *International Journal of Criminology and Penology* 5:129–57.

————. 1984. "Sex and violence: A ripple effect." Pp. 143–72 in N. Malamuth and E. Donnerstein (eds.), *Pornography and Sexual Aggression*. Orlando, FL: Academic Press.

Davis, Angela. 1981. *Women, Race and Class*. New York: Random House.

Davis, James A. and Tom W. Smith. 1986. *General Social Survey: Cumulative Codebook*. Chicago: National Opinion Research Center, University of Chicago.

DeCew, Judith Wagner. 1984. "Violent pornography: censorship, morality and social alternatives." *Journal of Applied Philosophy* 1:79–94.

Deevy, Sharon. 1975. "Such a nice girl." Pp. 21–26 in N. Myron and C. Bunch (eds.), *Lesbianism and the Women's Movement*. Baltimore: Diana Press.

Delacoste, Frederique and Priscilla Alexander. 1988. *Sex Work: Writings by Women in the Sex Industry*. Pittsburg: Cleis Press.

Dermer, Marshall and Thomas A. Pyszczynski. 1978. "Effects of erotica upon men's loving and liking responses for women they love." *Journal of Personality and Social Psychology* 36:1302–09.

Di Lauro, Al and Gerald Rabkin. 1976. *Dirty Movies: An Illustrated History of the Stag Film, 1915–1970*. New York: Chelsea House.

Diamond, Irene. 1980. "Pornography and repression: A reconsideration." *Signs* 5:686–701.

Diamond, Irene and Lee Quinby. 1984. "American feminism and the age of the body." *Signs* 10:119–25.

Dietz, Park and Barbara Evans. 1982. "Pornographic imagery and prevalence of paraphilia." *American Journal of Psychiatry* 19:1493–95.

Dietz, Park, Bruce Harry, and Robert R. Hazelwood. 1986. "Detective magazines: Pornography for the sexual sadist?" *Journal of Forensic Sciences* 31:197–211.

Donnerstein, Edward. 1980. "Aggressive erotica and violence against women." *Journal of Personality and Social Psychology* 39:269–77.

———. 1984. "Pornography: Its effects on violence against women." Pp. 53–82 in N. Malamuth and E. Donnerstein (eds.), *Pornography and Sexual Aggression*. Orlando, FL: Academic Press.

Donnerstein, Edward and Leonard Berkowitz. 1981. "Victim reactions in aggressive erotic films as a factor in violence against women." *Journal of Personality and Social Psychology* 41:710–24.

Donnerstein, Edward, Leonard Berkowitz, and Daniel Linz. 1986. "Role of aggressive and sexual images in violent pornography." Unpublished manuscript, University of Wisconsin-Madison.

Donnerstein, Edward, Marcia Donnerstein, and Ronald Evans. 1975. "Erotic stimuli and aggression: Facilitation or inhibition." *Journal of Personality and Social Psychology* 32:237–44.

Donnerstein, Edward and Daniel G. Linz. 1986a. "The question of pornography." *Psychology Today* (December):56–59.

————. 1986b. "Mass media sexual violence and male viewers: Current theory and research." *American Behavioral Scientist* 29:601–18.

Donnerstein, Edward, Daniel G. Linz, and Steven Penrod. 1987. *The Question of Pornography: Research Findings and Policy Implications.* New York: Free Press.

Douglas, Carol Anne. 1986. "Pornography: The Meese report." *Off Our Backs* (August-September):4–5.

Douglass v. Hustler Magazine, Inc., 769 F.2d 856 (1986).

Downey, Gary L. 1986. "Ideology and the Clamshell identity: Organizational dilemmas in the anti-nuclear power movement." *Social Problems* 33:357–73.

Downs, Donald Alexander. 1985. *Nazis in Skokie: Freedom, Community, and the First Amendment.* Notre Dame, IN: University of Notre Dame.

————. 1989. *The New Politics of Pornography.* Chicago: University of Chicago Press.

Duggan, Lisa. 1989. "What pornography means." *Women's Review of Books* (December):17–18.

Duggan, Lisa, Nan Hunter, and Carole S. Vance. 1985. "False promises: Feminist antipornography legislation in the U.S." Pp. 130–51 in V. Burstyn (ed.), *Women Against Censorship.* Vancouver: Douglas and McIntyre.

Duggan, Lisa and Ann Snitow. 1984. "Porn law is about images, not power." *Newsday* (September 26):65.

Durham III, Alexis M. 1986. "Pornography, social harm, and legal control: Observations on Bart." *Justice Quarterly* 3:95–102.

Dworkin, Andrea. 1981. *Pornography: Men Possessing Women.* New York: Perigee.

————. 1983. *Right-Wing Women.* New York: Perigee.

————. 1984. "Pornography: the new terrorism." Lecture presented at the conference, Pornography: Through the Eyes of Women. Madison, Wisconsin.

————. 1985. "Against the male flood: Censorship, pornography, and equality." *Harvard Women's Law Journal* 8:1–30.

————. 1987. *Intercourse.* New York: Free Press.

Dworkin, Andrea and Catharine A. MacKinnon. 1988. *Pornography and Civil Rights: A New Day for Women's Equality.* Minneapolis: Organizing Against Pornography.

Easterbrook, Judge Frank. 1989. "Pornography and the first amendment." Pp. 206–13 in M. E. Katsh (ed.), *Taking Sides: Clashing Views on Controversial Legal Issues,* third edition. Guilford, CT: Dushkin.

Ehrenreich, Barbara, Elizabeth Hess, and Gloria Jacobs. 1986. *Re-Making Love: The Feminization of Sex.* New York: Doubleday.

Eichelberger, Brenda. 1979. "Voices on black feminism." Pp. 225–31 in E. Shapiro and B. M. Shapiro (eds.), *The Women Say; The Men Say.* New York: Dell.

Einsiedel, Edna. 1989. "Social science and public policy: Looking at the 1986 Commission on Pornography." Pp. 87–107 in S. Gubar and J. Hoff (eds.), *For Adult Users Only: The Dilemma of Violent Pornography.* Bloomington: Indiana University Press.

Eitzen, D. Stanley. 1984. "Teaching social problems." *Society for the Study of Social Problems Newsletter* 16:10–11.

Ellis, Kate. 1985. "No sexuality without representation: A feminist view." *Changing Men* 15:13–14.

Ellis, Kate, Barbara O'Dair, and Abby Talmer (eds.). 1986. *Caught Looking.* New York: Caught Looking Inc.

Elmer, Jonathan. 1988. "The exciting conflict: The rhetoric of pornography and anti-pornography." *Cultural Critique* (Winter):45–77.

Emerson, Thomas I. 1985. "Censoring pornography would violate civil rights." Pp. 182–7 in D. Bender (ed.), *Should Pornography Be Censored?* St. Paul: Greenhaven Press.

English, Deirdre. 1980. "The politics of porn: Can feminists walk the line?" *Mother Jones* 5:20–23, 43–50.

Farrell, Warren. 1986. *Why Men Are the Way They Are.* New York: McGraw-Hill.

Ferguson, Ann. 1984. "Sex war: The debate between radical and libertarian feminists." *Signs* 10:106–12.

Fibreboard Paper Products Corp. v. NLRB, 379 U.S. 204 (1964).

Foucault, Michel. 1980. *The History of Sexuality*, trans. Robert Hurley. New York: Pantheon.

Freedman, Estelle and Barrie Thorne. 1984. "Introduction to 'the feminist sexuality debates'." *Signs* 10:102–5.

Friday, Nancy. 1974. *My Secret Garden*. New York: Pocket Books.

Furstenberg, Frank F., Kristin A. Moore, and James L. Peterson. 1985. "Sex education and sexual experience among adolescents." *American Journal of Public Health* 75:1331–32.

Gamson, William A. 1975. *The Strategy of Social Protest*. Homewood, IL: Dorsey Press.

Garcia, Alma M. 1989. "The development of Chicana feminist discourse, 1970–1980." *Gender and Society* 3:217–38.

Gardner, Tracey A. 1980. "Racism in pornography and the women's movement." Pp. 105–14 in L. Lederer (ed.), *Take Back the Night*. New York: Morrow.

Geertz, Clifford. 1975. "Common sense as a cultural system." *Antioch Review* 33:5–26.

Gerlach, Luther P. and Virginia H. Hine. 1970. *People, Power, and Change*. Indianapolis: Bobbs-Merrill.

Gieryn, Thomas. 1983. "Boundary-work and the demarcation of science from non-science: Strains and interests in professional ideologies of scientists." *American Sociological Review* 48:392–409.

Giles, Dennis. 1977. "Pornographic space: The other place." Pp. 52–65 in *The 1977 Film Studies Annual: Part 2*. Pleasantville, NY: Redgrave.

Gillespie, Dair L. and Ann Leffler. 1987. "The politics of research methodology in claims-making activities: Social science and sexual harassment." *Social Problems* 34:490–501.

Ginsberg v. New York, 390 U.S. 629 (1968).

Gitlin, Todd. 1990. "The left and porno." Pp. 102–4 in M. Kimmel (ed.), *Men Confront Pornography*. New York: Crown Books.

Goodchilds, Jacqueline and Gail Zellman. 1984. "Sexual signaling and sexual aggression in adolescent relationships." Pp. 233–43 in N. Malamuth and E. Donnerstein (eds.), *Pornography and Sexual Aggression*. Orlando, FL: Academic Press.

Gordon, Bettie. 1984. "Variety: The pleasure in looking." Pp. 189–203 in C. Vance (ed.), *Pleasure and Danger: Exploring Female Sexuality*. Boston: Routledge and Kegan Paul.

Gottdiener, M. 1985. "Hegemony and mass culture: A semiotic approach." *American Journal of Sociology* 90:979–1001.

Gray, Susan H. 1982. "Exposure to pornography and aggression toward women: The case of the angry male." *Social Problems* 29:387–98.

Greschner, Donna. 1985. "Book Review" of V. Burstyn's *Women Against Censorship. Resources for Feminist Research* 13:66–76.

Griffin, Susan. 1981. *Pornography and Silence: Culture's Revenge Against Nature.* New York: Harper and Row.

Gross, Daniel. 1990. "The gender rap." *The New Republic* (April 16):11–14.

Guerrieri, Dexter. 1985. "Pornography and silent men." *Changing Men* 15:9–10.

Gusfield, Joseph. 1963. *Symbolic Crusade: Status Politics and the American Temperance Movement.* Chicago: University of Illinois Press.

Haug, F. W. 1986. *Critique of Commodity Aesthetics: Appearance, Sexuality, and Advertising in Capitalist Society,* trans. R. Bock. Minneapolis: University of Minnesota Press.

Hawkins, Gordon and Franklin E. Zimring. 1988. *Pornography in a Free Society.* Cambridge, MA: Cambridge University Press.

Hazelrigg, Lawrence E. 1986. "Is there a choice between 'constructionism' and 'objectivism'?" *Social Problems* 6:S1–S13.

Hazen, Helen. 1983. *Endless Rapture: Rape, Romance, and the Female Imagination.* New York: Charles Scribner.

Herman, Judith. 1988. "Considering sex offenders: A model of addiction." *Signs* 13:695–724.

Herrman, Margaret S. and Diane C. Bordner. 1983. "Attitudes toward pornography in a southern community." *Criminology* 21:349–74.

Hertzberg, Hendrik. 1986. "Big boobs: Ed Meese and his pornography commission." *The New Republic* (July 14):21–24.

Hilgartner, Stephen and Charles L. Bosk. 1988. "The rise and fall of social problems: A public arenas model." *American Journal of Sociology* 94:53–78.

Hilker, Anne K. 1979. "Tort liability of the media for audience acts of violence: A constitutional analysis." *Southern California Law Review* 52:529–71.

Hite, Shere. 1976. *The Hite Report*. New York: Macmillan.

Hoff, Joan. 1989. "Why is there no history of pornography?" Pp. 17–46 in S. Gubar and J. Hoff (eds.), *For Adult Users Only: The Dilemma of Violent Pornography*. Bloomington: Indiana University Press.

Holquist, Michael. 1983. "The politics of representation." *The Quarterly Newsletter of the Laboratory of Comparative Human Cognition* 5:2–9.

Hooks, Bell. 1981. *Ain't I a Woman: Black Women and Feminism*. Boston: South End Press.

Horowitz, Gad and Michael Kaufman. 1987. "Male sexuality: Toward a theory of liberation." In M. Kaufman (ed.), *Beyond Patriarchy: Essays by Men on Pleasure, Power, and Change*. Toronto: Oxford.

Hunt, Alan. 1985. "The ideology of law: Advances and problems in recent applications of the concept of ideology to the analysis of law." *Law and Society Review* 19:11–37.

Hunter, Nan D. and Sylvia A. Law. 1985. Brief Amici Curiae of Feminist Anti-Censorship Task Force to U.S. Court of Appeals for the Seventh Circuit Court, *American Booksellers, Inc. v. Hudnut*.

Intons-Peterson, Margaret and Beverly Roskos-Ewoldsen. 1989. "Mitigating the effects of violent pornography." Pp. 218–39 in S. Gubar and J. Hoff (eds.), *For Adult Users Only: The Dilemma of Violent Pornography*. Bloomington: Indiana University Press.

Irigaray, Luce. 1985. *This Sex Which Is Not One*, trans. C. Porter and C. Burke. Ithaca, NY: Cornell University Press.

Jackson, Stevie. 1978. "The social context of rape: Sexual scripts and motivation." *Women's Studies International Quarterly* 1:27–38.

Jacobellis v. Ohio, 378 U.S. 184 (1964).

Jaggar, Alison M. 1983. *Feminist Politics and Human Nature*. Totowa, NJ: Rowman and Allanheld.

Jenkins v. Georgia, 418 U.S. 153 (1974).

Jones, Ann. 1980. *Women Who Kill*. New York: Fawcett.

Jones, Elise F., Jacqueline D. Forrest, Noreen Goldman, Stanley K. Henshaw, Richard Lincoln, Jeannie I. Rossoff, Charles F. Westoff, and Deirdre Wulf. 1985. "Teenage pregnancy in developed countries: Determinants and policy implications." *Family Planning Perspectives* 17:53–69.

Kairys, David. 1982. "Freedom of speech." Pp. 140–71 in D. Kairys (ed.), *The Politics of Law*. New York: Pantheon.

Kaminer, Wendy. 1980. "Pornography and the first amendment: Prior restraints and private action." Pp. 241–47 in L. Lederer (ed.), *Take Back the Night*. New York: Morrow.

———. 1990. *A Fearful Freedom: Women's Flight from Equality*. Reading, MA: Addison-Wesley.

Kaplan, E. Ann. 1983a. "Is the gaze male?" Pp. 309–27 in A. Snitow, C. Stansell, and S. Thompson (eds.), *Powers of Desire: The Politics of Sexuality*. New York: Monthly Review Press.

———. 1983b. *Women and Film: Both Sides of the Camera*. New York: Methuen.

Kappeler, Susanne. 1986. *The Pornography of Representation*. Minneapolis: University of Minnesota Press.

Kendrick, Walter. 1987. *The Secret Museum: Pornography in Modern Culture*. New York: Viking Press.

Kenrick, Douglas T. and Sara E. Gutierres. 1980. "Contrast effects and judgments of physical attractiveness: When beauty becomes a social problem." *Journal of Personality and Social Psychology* 38:131–40.

Kimmel, Michael S. 1987a. "The contemporary 'crisis' in masculinity in historical perspective." Pp. 121–53 in H. Brod (ed.), *The Making of Masculinities*. Boston: Allen and Unwin.

——— (ed.). 1987b. *Changing Men: New Directions in Research on Men and Masculinity*. Newbury Park, CA: Sage.

———. 1987c. "Men's responses to feminism at the turn of the century." *Gender and Society* 1:261–83.

——— (ed.). 1990. *Men Confront Pornography*. New York: Crown Books.

Kimmel, Michael S. and Michael A. Messner (eds.). 1989. *Men's Lives*. New York: Macmillan.

Kirkpatrick, R. George and Louis A. Zurcher. 1983. "Women against pornography: Feminist anti-pornography crusades in American Society." *International Journal of Sociology and Social Policy* 3:1–30.

Klatch, Rebecca E. 1987. *Women of the New Right*. Philadelphia: Temple University Press.

Koss, Mary, Christine A. Gidycz, and Nadine Wisniewski. 1987. "The scope of rape: Incidence and prevalence of sexual aggression in a national sample of higher education students." *Journal of Consulting and Clinical Psychology* 55:162–70.

Koss, Mary, Kenneth E. Leonard, Dana Beezley, and Cheryl J. Oros. 1985. "Nonstranger sexual aggression: A discriminant analysis of the psychological characteristics of undetected offenders." *Sex Roles* 12:981–92.

Kovel, Joel. 1990. "The antidialectic of pornography." Pp. 153–67 in M. Kimmel (ed.), *Men Confront Pornography*. New York: Crown Books.

Krafka, Carol L. 1985. *Sexually Explicit, Sexually Violent, and Violent Media: Effects of Multiple Naturalistic Exposures and Debriefing on Female Viewers*. Ph.D. dissertation, University of Wisconsin-Madison.

Krampen, Martin. 1979. *Meaning in the Urban Environment*. London: Pion.

Kutchinsky, Berl. 1973. "The effect of easy availability of pornography on the incidence of sex crimes: The Danish experience." *Journal of Social Issues* 29:163–81.

———. 1983. "Obscenity and pornography: Behavioral aspects." Pp. 1077–86 in S. Kadish (ed.), *Encyclopedia of Crime and Justice*, Volume 3. New York: Free Press.

———. 1985. "Pornography and its effects in Denmark and the United States: A rejoinder and beyond." *Comparative Social Research* 8:301–30.

LaFree, Gary D. 1989. *Rape and Criminal Justice: The Social Construction of Sexual Assault*. Belmont, CA: Wadsworth.

LaHaye, Tim and Beverly LaHaye. 1976. *The Act of Marriage: The Beauty of Sexual Love*. Grand Rapids, MI: Zondervan.

Lederer, Laura (ed.). 1980. *Take Back the Night: Women on Pornography*. New York: Morrow.

Leidholdt, Dorchen. 1983. "Fighting woman-hating ads." *Newsreport of Women Against Pornography* 5:1, 6–7.

Leo, John. 1987. "Romantic porn in boudoir." *Time* (March 30):63–64.

Lerner, Gerda. 1986. *The Creation of Patriarchy*. New York: Oxford University Press.

Leventhal, Harold. 1977. "An empirical inquiry into the effect of *Miller v. California* on the control of obscenity." *New York University Law Review* 52:810–939.

156   REFERENCES

Linden, Robin R., Darlene R. Pagano, Diana E. H. Russell, and Susan L.
    Star (eds.). 1982. *Against Sadomasochism: A Radical Feminist
    Analysis*. Palo Alto, CA: Frog in the Well Press.
Linz, Daniel. 1985. *Sexual Violence in the Media: Effects on Male View-
    ers and Implications for Society*. Ph.D. dissertation, University
    of Wisconsin-Madison.
Linz, Daniel, Edward Donnerstein, and Steven Penrod. 1984. "The ef-
    fects of multiple exposures to filmed violence against women."
    Journal of Communication 34:130–47.
———. 1988. "Effects of long-term exposure to violent and sexually
    degrading depictions of women." *Journal of Personality and
    Social Psychology* 55:758–68.
Linz, Daniel, Charles W. Turner, Bradford W. Hesse, and Steven
    D. Penrod. 1984. "Bases of liability for injuries produced by
    media portrayals of violent pornography." Pp. 277–304 in N.
    Malamuth and E. Donnerstein (eds.), *Pornography and Sexual
    Aggression*. Orlando, FL: Academic Press.
Lippert, John. 1977. "Sexuality as consumption." Pp. 207–13 in J.
    Snodgrass (ed.), *For Men Against Sexism*. Albion, CA: Times
    Change Press.
Litewka, Jack. 1977. "The socialized penis." Pp. 16–35 in J. Snodgrass
    (ed.), *For Men Against Sexism*. Albion, CA: Times Change
    Press.
Lobel, Kerry. 1986. *Naming the Violence: Speaking Out About Lesbian
    Battering*. Seattle: Seal Press.
Longino, Helen E. 1980. "Pornography, oppression, and freedom: A
    closer look." Pp. 40–54 in L. Lederer (ed.), *Take Back the
    Night*. New York: Morrow.
Lopate, Phillip. 1981. *Bachelorhood*. Boston: Little, Brown.
Lord, Charles C., Lee Ross, and Mark R. Lepper. 1979. "Biased assimi-
    lation and attitude to polarization: The effects of prior theories
    on subsequently considered evidence." *Journal of Personality
    and Social Psychology* 37:2098–2109.
Lovelace, Linda and Mike McGrady. 1980. *Ordeal*. New York: Berkley
    Books.
Lukacs, Georg. 1971. *History and Class Consciousness: Studies in
    Marxist Dialectics*, trans. R. Livingston. Cambridge: MIT Press.
Lyman, Peter. 1987. "The fraternal bond as a joking relationship: A
    case study of the role of sexist jokes in male group bonding."

Pp. 148–63 in M. Kimmel (ed.), *Changing Men.* Newbury Park, CA: Sage.

Lynn, Barry W. and Al Goldstein. 1985. "Pornography should not be censored." Pp. 182–7 in D. Bender (ed.), *Should Pornography Be Censored?* St. Paul: Greenhaven Press.

MacDonald, Scott. 1990. "Confessions of a feminist porn watcher." Pp. 34–42 in M. Kimmel (ed.), *Men Confront Pornography.* New York: Crown Books.

MacKinnon, Catharine. 1979. *Sexual Harassment of Working Women.* New Haven: Yale University Press.

———. 1982. "Feminism, Marxism, method, and the state: An agenda for theory." *Signs* 7:515–44.

———. 1983. "Feminism, Marxism, method, and the state: Toward feminist jurisprudence." *Signs* 8:635–58.

———. 1984. "Not a moral issue." *Yale Law and Policy Review* 2:321–45.

———. 1985. "An open letter to Adrienne Rich." *Off Our Backs* (October):18.

———. 1986. "Pornography as sex discrimination." *Law and Inequality* 4:38–49.

———. 1987. *Feminism Unmodified: Discourses on Life and Law.* Cambridge, MA: Harvard University Press.

Macridis, Roy C. 1983. *Contemporary Political Ideologies: Movements and Regimes.* Boston: Little, Brown.

Malamuth, Neil M. 1981a. "Rape proclivity among males." *Journal of Social Issues* 37:138–57.

———. 1981b. "Rape fantasies as a function of exposure to violent sexual stimuli." *Archives of Sexual Behavior* 10:33–47.

———. 1983. "Factors associated with rape as predictors of laboratory aggression against women." *Journal of Personality and Social Psychology* 45:432–42.

———. 1984. "Aggression against women: Cultural and individual causes." Pp. 19–52 in N. Malamuth and E. Donnerstein (eds.), *Pornography and Sexual Aggression.* Orlando, FL: Academic Press.

———. 1985. "The mass media and aggression against women: Research findings and prevention." Pp. 392–412 in A. W. Burgess (ed.), *Rape and Sexual Assault: A Research Handbook.* New York: Garland.

Malamuth, Neil M. and James V. P. Check. 1980a. "Penile tumescence and perceptual responses to rape as a function of victim's perceived reactions." *Journal of Applied Social Psychology* 10:528–47.

———. 1980b. "Sexual arousal to rape and consenting depictions: The importance of the woman's arousal." *Journal of Abnormal Psychology* 89:763–6.

———. 1981. "The effects of mass media exposure on acceptance of violence against women: A field experiment." *Journal of Research in Personality* 15:436–46.

———. 1984. "Debriefing effectiveness following exposure to pornographic rape depictions." *Journal of Sex Research* 20:1–13.

———. 1985. "The effects of aggressive pornography on beliefs in rape myths: Individual differences." *Journal of Research in Personality* 19:299–320.

Malamuth, Neil M., Maggie Heim, and Seymour Feshbach. 1980. "Sexual responsiveness of college students to rape depictions: Inhibitory and disinhibitory effects." *Journal of Personality and Social Psychology* 38:399–408.

Malamuth, Neil M. and Barry Spinner. 1980. "A longitudinal content analysis of sexual violence in best-selling erotic magazines." *Journal of Sex Research* 16:226–37.

Mansbridge, Jane J. 1986. *Why We Lost the ERA*. Chicago: University of Chicago Press.

Manual Enterprises v. Day, 370 U.S. 478 (1962).

Marcus, Steven. 1974. *The Other Victorians: A Study of Sexuality and Pornography in Mid-Nineteenth Century England*. New York: New American Library.

Marcuse, Herbert. 1964. *One Dimensional Man*. Boston: Beacon Press.

———. 1969. "Repressive tolerance." Pp. 81–123 in R. Wolff, B. Moore, and H. Marcuse, *A Critique of Pure Tolerance*. Boston: Beacon Press.

Marshall, Susan E. 1989. "Keep us on the pedestal: Women against feminism in twentieth-century America." Pp. 567–80 in J. Freeman (ed.), *Women: A Feminist Perspective*, fourth edition. Mountain View, CA: Mayfield.

Martin, Patricia Yancey and Robert A. Hummer. 1989. "Fraternities and rape on campus." *Gender and Society* 3:457–73.

Marx, Karl. 1967 [1867]. *Capital, Volume 1: The Process of Capitalist*

Production, trans. S. Moore and E. Aveling. New York: International Publishers.

Masters, William H. and Virginia E. Johnson. 1966. *The Human Sexual Response*. Boston: Little, Brown.

Mathews, Tom. 1990. "Fine art or foul?" *Newsweek* (July 2):46–52.

McCarthy, Sarah J. 1980. "Pornography, rape, and the cult of macho." *The Humanist* (September/October):11–20.

McConahay, John. 1988. "Pornography: The symbolic politics of fantasy." *Law and Contemporary Problems* 51:31–69.

McCormack, Thelma. 1978. "Machismo in media research: A critical review of research on violence and pornography." *Social Problems* 25:544–55.

———. 1985a. "Feminism and the first amendment." *Justice Quarterly* 2:271–82.

———. 1985b. "Making sense of the research on pornography." Pp. 183–205 in V. Burstyn (ed.), *Women Against Censorship*. Vancouver: Douglas and McIntyre.

Mehan, Hugh and John Wills. 1988. "MEND: A nurturing voice in the nuclear arms debate." *Social Problems* 4:363–83.

Men Against Pornography. 1990. "Is pornography jerking you around?" Pp. 293–6 in M. Kimmel (ed.), *Men Confront Pornography*. New York: Crown Books.

Meritor Savings Bank, FSB v. Vinson, 54 U.S.L.W. 4703 (1986).

Messerschmidt, James W. 1986. *Capitalism, Patriarchy, and Crime: Toward a Socialist Feminist Criminology*. Totowa, NJ: Rowman and Littlefield.

Mill, John Stuart. 1961. "On liberty." Pp. 185–319 in M. Cohen (ed.), *The Philosophy of John Stuart Mill*. New York: Modern Library.

Miller v. California, 413 U.S. 15 (1973).

Minnery, Tom. 1986. "Pornography: The human tragedy." *Christianity Today* (March 7):7.

Morgan, Marabel. 1973. *The Total Woman*. Old Tappan, NJ: Felming H. Revell.

Morgan, Robin. 1978. "How to run pornographers out of town and preserve the first amendment." *Ms.* (November):55, 78–80.

———. 1980. "Theory and practice: Pornography and rape." Pp. 134–40 in L. Lederer (ed.), *Take Back the Night*. New York: Morrow.

Mosher, Donald L. and Ronald D. Anderson. 1986. "Macho personality, sexual aggression, and reactions to guided imagery of realistic rape." *Journal of Research in Personality* 20:77–94.

Mura, David. 1987. *A Male Grief: Notes on Pornography and Addiction*. Minneapolis: Milkweed Editions.

New York v. Ferber, 458 U.S. 747 (1982).

New York Times v. Sullivan, 376 U.S. 255 (1964).

Nicholson, Linda. 1989. "A radical's odyssey." *Women's Review of Books* (December):11–12.

O'Brien, Shirley. 1983. *Child Pornography*. Dubuque, IA: Kendall/Hunt.

Osanka, Franklin Mark and Sara Lee Johann. 1989. *Sourcebook on Pornography*. Lexington, MA: Lexington Books.

Page, Ann L. and Donald A. Clelland. 1978. "The Kanawha County textbook controversy: A study of the politics of life style concern." *Social Forces* 57:265–81.

Palys, T. S. 1986. "Testing the common wisdom: The social content of video pornography." *Canadian Psychology* 27:22–35.

Papandreou, Margarita. 1988. "Feminism and political power: Some thoughts on a strategy for the future." Pp. xi–xix in E. Boneparth and E. Stoper (eds.), *Women, Power, and Policy: Toward the Year 2000*. New York: Pergamon Press.

Penrod, Steven and Daniel Linz. 1984. "Using psychological research on violent pornography to inform legal change." Pp. 247–75 in N. Malamuth and E. Donnerstein (eds.), *Pornography and Sexual Aggression*. Orlando, FL: Academic Press.

Pfohl, Stephen J. 1977. "The 'discovery' of child abuse." *Social Problems* 24:310–23.

Philipson, Ilene. 1984. "The repression of history and gender: A critical perspective on the feminist sexuality debate." *Signs* 10:113–8.

Pleck, Joseph. 1989. "Men's power with women, other men, and society: A men's movement analysis." Pp. 21–29 in M. Kimmel and M. Messner (eds.), *Men's Lives*. New York: Macmillan.

Pope v. Illinois, 107 S.Ct. 1918 (1987).

Prince, Stephen. 1987. "Power, pleasure, and pain in pornographic feature films." Paper presented at the annual International Communication Association conference.

Quinney, Richard. 1989. "The problem of suffering: Social problems and the way of peace." Pp. 95–105 in J. Holstein and G. Miller (eds.), *Perspectives on Social Problems*, Volume 1. Greenwich, CT: JAI Press.

Rafter, Nicole Hahn and Elena M. Natalizia. 1981. "Marxist feminism: Implications for criminal justice." *Crime and Delinquency* 27:81–98.

Randall, Richard S. 1989. *Freedom and Taboo: Pornography and the Politics of the Divided Self.* Berkeley: University of California Press.

Regina V. Hicklin, L. R. 3 Q. B. (1868).

Reich, Wilhelm. 1972. *Sex-Pol: Essays 1929–1937*, ed. L. Baxandall. New York: Random House.

Renton v. Playtime Theatres, Inc., 475 U.S. 41 (1986).

Rich, Adrienne. 1980. "Afterword." Pp. 313–20 in L. Lederer (ed.), *Take Back the Night*. New York: Morrow.

———. 1985. "We don't have to come apart over pornography." *Off Our Backs* (July):30.

Robel, Lauren. 1989. "Pornography and existing law: What the law can do." Pp. 178–97 in S. Gubar and J. Hoff (eds.), *For Adult Users Only: The Dilemma of Violent Pornography*. Bloomington: Indiana University Press.

Roe v. Wade, 410 U.S. 113 (1973).

Rose, Vicki McNickle. 1977. "Rape as a social problem: A by-product of the feminist movement." *Social Problems* 25:75–89.

Roth v. United States, 354 U.S. 476 (1957).

Rubenstein, Carin and Carol Tavris. 1987. "Survey Results." *Redbook* (September):147–9, 214–5.

Rubin, Gayle, Deirdre English, and Amber Hollibaugh. 1981. "Talking Sex: A conversation on sexuality and feminism." *Socialist Review* 11:43–62.

Russell, Diana E. H. 1980. "Pornography and the women's liberation movement." Pp. 301–6 in L. Lederer (ed.), *Take Back the Night*. New York: Morrow.

———. 1982. *Rape in Marriage*. New York: Collier Books.

———. 1984. *Sexual Exploitation: Rape, Child Sexual Abuse, and Workplace Harassment*. Beverly Hills, CA: Sage.

Russo, Ann. 1987. "Conflicts and contradictions among feminists over issues of pornography and sexual freedom." *Women's Studies International Forum* 10:103–12.

Ryan, Barbara. 1989. "Ideological purity and feminism: The U.S.

women's movement from 1966 to 1975." *Gender and Society* 3:239–57.

Sadella, Edward K., Douglas T. Kenrick, and Beth Vershure. 1987. "Dominance and heterosexual attraction." *Journal of Personality and Social Psychology* 52:730–8.

Sanday, Peggy Reeves. 1981. *Female Power and Male Dominance: On the Origins of Sexual Inequality*. New York: Cambridge University Press.

Schipper, Henry. 1980. "Filthy lucre: A tour of America's most profitable frontier." *Mother Jones* 5:31–33, 60–62.

Schwendinger, Julia R. and Herman Schwendinger. 1983. *Rape and Inequality*. Beverly Hills, CA: Sage.

Scott, David Alexander. 1985. *Pornography: Its Effects on the Family, Community and Culture*. Washington, DC: Free Congress Foundation.

Scott, Joseph E. 1986. "An updated longitudinal content analysis of sex references in mass circulation magazines." *Journal of Sex Research* 22:16–23.

Scott, Joseph E. and Steven J. Cuvelier. 1987. "Sexual violence in *Playboy* magazine: A longitudinal analysis." *Journal of Sex Research* 23:534–9.

Scott, Joseph E. and Loretta A. Schwalm. 1988a. "Pornography and rape: An examination of adult theater rates by state." Pp. 40–53 in J. Scott and T. Hirschi (eds.), *Controversial Issues in Crime and Justice*. Newbury Park, CA: Sage.

———. 1988b. "Rape rates and the circulation rates of adult magazines." *Journal of Sex Research* 24:241–50.

Scully, Diana and Joseph Marolla. 1984. "Convicted rapists' vocabulary of motives: Excuses and justifications." *Social Problems* 31:530–44.

Searles, Patricia and Ronald J. Berger. 1987. "The feminist self-defense movement: A case study." *Gender and Society* 1:61–83.

Sears, David O. 1986. "College sophomores in the laboratory: Influence of a narrow data base on social psychology's view of human nature." *Journal of Personality and Social Psychology* 51:515–30.

Sheinfeld, Lois. 1985. "The first amendment forbids censorship." Pp. 182–7 in D. Bender (ed.), *Should Pornography Be Censored?* St. Paul: Greenhaven Press.

Simmel, Georg. 1971 [1908]. *Georg Simmel: On Individual and Social Forms, Selected Writings*, ed. D. Levine. Chicago: University of Chicago Press.

Simon, William. 1990. "Testing freedom and restraint." Pp. 297–304 in M. Kimmel (ed.), *Men Confront Pornography*. New York: Crown Books.

Skidmore, Max J. 1989. *Ideologies: Politics in Action*. San Diego: Harcourt Brace Jovanovich.

Slade, Joseph. 1984. "Violence in the hard-core pornographic film: An historical survey." *Journal of Communication* 34:148–63.

Small, Fred. 1985. "Pornography and censorship." *Changing Men* 15:7–8, 43–45.

Smith, Donald D. 1976. "The social content of pornography." *Journal of Communication* 26:16–33.

Smith, Dorothy. 1979. "A sociology of women." Pp. 135–87 in J. Sherman and E. Beck (eds.), *The Prism of Sex: Essays in the Sociology of Knowledge*. Madison: University of Wisconsin Press.

Smith, Tom W. 1987. "The use of public opinion data by the Attorney General's Commission on Pornography." *Public Opinion Quarterly* 51:249–67.

Snitow, Ann Barr. 1983. "Mass market romance: Pornography for women is different." Pp. 245–63 in A. Snitow, C. Stansell, and S. Thompson (eds.), *Powers of Desire: The Politics of Sexuality*. New York: Monthly Review Press.

———. 1985. "Retrenchment versus transformation: The politics of the antipornography movement." Pp. 107–20 in V. Burstyn (ed.), *Women Against Censorship*. Vancouver: Douglas and McIntyre.

Soble, Alan. 1986. *Pornography: Marxism, Feminism, and the Future of Sexuality*. New Haven, CT: Yale University Press.

Sontag, Susan. 1973. *On Pornography*. New York: Farrar, Straus and Giroux.

Spector, Malcolm and John I. Kitsuse. 1977. *Constructing Social Problems*. Menlo Park, CA: Cummings.

Squire, Susan. 1985. "How women are changing porn films." *Glamour* (November):282–83.

Stacey, Judith and Barrie Thorne. 1985. "The missing feminist revolution in sociology." *Social Problems* 32:301–16.

Staggenborg, Suzanne. 1986. "Coalition work in the pro-choice movement: Organizational and environmental opportunities and obstacles." *Social Problems* 33:374–90.

———. 1988. "Consequences of professionalization and formalization in the pro-choice movement." *American Sociological Review* 53:585–605.

Stanley v. Georgia, 394 U.S. 557 (1969).

Staples, Robert. 1990. "Blacks and pornography: A different response." Pp. 111–4 in M. Kimmel (ed.), *Men Confront Pornography*. New York: Crown Books.

Steele, Lisa. 1985. "A capital idea: Gendering in the mass media." Pp. 58–78 in V. Burstyn (ed.), *Women Against Censorship*. Vancouver: Douglas and McIntrye.

Steinberg, David. 1990. "The roots of pornography." Pp. 54–59 in M. Kimmel (ed.), *Men Confront Pornography*. New York: Crown Books.

Steinem, Gloria. 1980. "Erotica and pornography: A clear and present difference." Pp. 35–39 in L. Lederer (ed.), *Take Back the Night*. New York: Morrow.

———. 1986. "The real Linda Lovelace." Pp. 274–85 in *Outrageous Acts and Everyday Rebellions*. New York: New American Library.

Stodder, Jim. 1979. "Confessions of a candy-ass roughneck." Pp. 40–41 in E. Shapiro and B. M. Shapiro (eds.), *The Women Say; The Men Say*. New York: Dell.

Stoltenberg, John. 1985. "Pornography and freedom." *Changing Men* 15:5–6, 46–7.

———. 1988. "You can't fight homophobia and protect the pornographers at the same time." *Changing Men* 19:11–13.

———. 1989. *Refusing to be a Man: Essays on Sex and Justice*. Portland: Breitenbush Books.

———. 1990. "Gays and the propornography movement: Having the hots for sex discrimination." Pp. 248–62 in M. Kimmel (ed.), *Men Confront Pornography*. New York: Crown Books.

Sumner, Colin. 1979. *Reading Ideologies: An Investigation into the Marxist Theory of Ideology*. London: Academic Press.

Sunstein, Cass R. 1986a. "Notes on pornography and the first amendment." *Law and Inequality* 4:28–38.

———. 1986b. "Pornography and the first amendment." *Duke Law Journal* (September):589–627.

Swidler, Ann. 1986. "Culture in action: Symbols and strategies." *American Sociological Review* 51:273–86.

Taub, Nadine and Elizabeth M. Schneider. 1982. "Perspectives on women's subordination and the law." Pp. 117–39 in D. Kairys (ed.), *The Politics of Law*. New York: Pantheon.

Taylor, Verta. 1983. "The future of feminism in the 1980s: A social movement analysis." Pp. 434–51 in L. Richardson and V. Taylor (eds.), *Feminist Frontiers: Rethinking Sex, Gender, and Society*. Reading, MA: Addison-Wesley.

Teish, Luisah. 1980. "A quiet subversion." Pp. 115–8 in L. Lederer (ed.), *Take Back the Night*. New York: Morrow.

Thompson, John B. 1984. *Studies in the Theory of Ideology*. Berkeley: University of California Press.

Thurston, Carol. 1987. *The Romance Revolution: Erotic Novels for Women and the Quest for a New Sexual Identity*. Urbana: University of Illinois Press.

Tiefer, Leonore. 1987. "In pursuit of the perfect penis: The medicalization of male sexuality." Pp. 165–84 in M. Kimmel (ed.), *Changing Men*. Newbury Park, CA: Sage.

Tierney, Kathleen J. 1982. "The battered women movement and the creation of the wife beating problem." *Social Problems* 29:207–20.

Tigue, Randall D. B. 1985. "Civil rights and censorship—Incompatible bedfellows." *William Mitchell Law Review* 11:81–125.

Time. 1986. "Pornography: A Poll." (July 21):22.

Tong, Rosemarie. 1984. *Women, Sex, and the Law*. Totowa, NJ: Rowman and Allanheld.

———. 1989. *Feminist Thought: A Comprehensive Introduction*. Boulder, CO: Westview Press.

Tucker, Kenneth H. 1989. "Ideology and social movements: The contributions of Habermas." *Sociological Inquiry* 59:30–47.

Tucker, Scott. 1990. "Radical feminism and gay male porn." Pp. 263–87 in M. Kimmel (ed.), *Men Confront Pornography*. New York: Crown Books.

Van Gelder, Lindsy. 1986. "Pornography goes to Washington: What can Reagan, Meese, the radical right, and feminists possibly have to say to each other about porn?" *Ms*. (April):52–54, 83.

Vance, Carole S. (ed.). 1984. *Pleasure and Danger: Exploring Female Sexuality*. Boston: Routledge and Kegan Paul.

————. 1986. "The Meese commission on the road." *The Nation* (August):76–80.

Vance, Carole S. and Ann Barr Snitow. 1984. "Toward a conversation about sex in feminism: A modest proposal." *Signs* 10:126–35.

Walker, Alice. 1980. "Coming apart." Pp. 95–104 in L. Lederer (ed.), *Take Back the Night*. New York: Morrow.

Walkowitz, Judith. 1980. *Prostitution and Victorian Society: Women, Class and the State*. Cambridge: Cambridge University Press.

Waring, Nancy W. 1986. "Coming to terms with pornography: Toward a feminist perspective on sex, censorship, and hysteria." *Research in Law, Deviance, and Social Control* 8:85–112.

Weaver, Mary Jo. 1989. "Pornography and the religious imagination." Pp. 68–86 in S. Gubar and J. Hoff (eds.), *For Adult Users Only: The Dilemma of Violent Pornography*. Bloomington: Indiana University Press.

Webster, Paula. 1981. "Pornography and pleasure." *Heresies* 3:48–51.

Weeks, Jeffrey. 1981. *Sex, Politics and Society: The Regulation of Sexuality Since 1800*. New York: Longman.

Weinstein, Jeff. 1990. "What porn did." Pp. 277–80 in M. Kimmel (ed.), *Men Confront Pornography*. New York: Crown Books.

Weis, Kurt and Sandra S. Borges. 1973. "Victimology and rape: The case of the legitimate victim." *Issues in Criminology* 8:71–115.

Weiss, Philip. 1990. "Forbidden pleasures." Pp. 91–98 in M. Kimmel (ed.), *Men Confront Pornography*. New York: Crown Books.

West, Robin. 1989. "Pornography as a legal text: Comments from a legal perspective." Pp. 108–30 in S. Gubar and J. Hoff (eds.), *For Adult Users Only: The Dilemma of Violent Pornography*. Bloomington: Indiana University Press.

White, Van F. 1985. "Pornography and pride." *Changing Men* 15:17–18.

Will, George F. 1990. "America's slide into the sewer." *Newsweek* (July 30):64.

Williams, Joyce E. and Karen A. Holmes. 1981. *The Second Assault: Rape and Public Attitudes*. Westport, CT: Greenwood Press.

Williams, Linda. 1989a. *Hard Core: Power, Pleasure, and the "Frenzy of the Visible."* Berkeley: University of California Press.

————. 1989b. "Fetishism and hard core: Marx, Freud, and the 'money shot'." Pp. 198–217 in S. Gubar and J. Hoff (eds.),

For Adult Users Only: The Dilemma of Violent Pornography. Bloomington: Indiana University Press.

Willis, Ellen. 1982a. "Toward a feminist sexual revolution." *Social Text* 6:3–21.

———. 1982b. "Who is a feminist?" *Village Voice Literary Supplement.* New York (December):16–17.

Wilson, Kenneth, Rebecca Faison, and G. M. Britton. 1983. "Cultural aspects of male sex aggression." *Deviant Behavior* 4:241–55.

Wilson, W. Cody. 1978. "Can pornography contribute to the prevention of sexual problems?" Pp. 159–79 in C. Qualls, J. Wincze, and D. Barlow (eds.), *The Prevention of Sexual Disorders: Issues and Approaches.* New York: Plenum.

Wolfe, Alan. 1990. "Dirt and democracy." *The New Republic* (February 19):27–31.

Wolin, Sheldon S. 1960. *Politics and Visions: Continuity and Innovation in Western Political Thought.* Boston: Little, Brown.

Wood, Michael and Michael Hughes. 1984. "The moral basis of moral reform: Status discontent vs. culture and socialization as explanations of anti-pornography social movement adherence." *American Sociological Review* 49:86–99.

Young v. American Mini Theatres, 427 U.S. 50 (1976).

Zabin, Laurie S., Marilyn F. Hirsch, Edward A. Smith, Rosalie Streett, and Janet B. Hardy. 1986. "Evaluation of a pregnancy prevention program for urban teenagers." *Family Planning Perspectives* 18:119–26.

Zilbergeld, Bernie. 1990. "Porn as therapy." Pp. 120–2 in M. Kimmel (ed.), *Men Confront Pornography.* New York: Crown Books.

Zillmann, Dolf and Jennings Bryant. 1982. "Pornography, sexual callousness, and the trivialization of rape." *Journal of Communication* 32:10–21.

———. 1984. "Effects of massive exposure to pornography." Pp. 115–38 in N. Malamuth and E. Donnerstein (eds.), *Pornography and Sexual Aggression.* Orlando, FL: Academic Press.

———. 1986. "Pornography's impact on sexual satisfaction." Unpublished manuscript, Indiana University, Bloomington.

Zillmann, Dolf, Jennings Bryant, Paul W. Comisky, and Norman J. Medoff. 1981. "Excitation and hedonic valence in the effect of erotica on motivated intermale aggression." *European Journal of Social Psychology* 11:233–52.

Zillmann, Dolf, James B. Weaver, Norbert Mundorf, and Charles F. Aust. 1986. "Effects of an opposite-gender companion's affect to horror on distress, delight, and attraction." *Journal of Personality and Social Psychology* 51:586–94.

Zurcher, Louis A. and R. George Kirkpatrick. 1976. *Citizens for Decency: Antipornography Crusades as Status Defense*. Austin: University of Texas Press.

Index

ABOUT THE AUTHORS

RONALD J. BERGER, Professor of Sociology and Coordinator of the Criminal Justice Program at the University of Wisconsin-Whitewater, teaches courses in criminology and the sociology of law.

PATRICIA SEARLES, Professor of Sociology and Women's Studies at the University of Wisconsin-Whitewater, teaches courses in gender roles, the family, and violence against women.

CHARLES E. COTTLE, Professor of Political Science at the University of Wisconsin-Whitewater, teaches courses in political theory, public opinion, and research methods.

Together or separately, they have published on a number of feminist and gender-related topics, including sexual assault, rape law reform, women's self-defense, female delinquency, media images of women, and pornography.